FROM **AIMLESS**
TO **AMAZING**

The Rewire Retirement Method

CYN MEYER

PRAISE FOR THE REWIRE RETIREMENT METHOD

"Give yourself the key to unlock what resonates for you at this stage of life."
—Theresa Fowler, Tulsa, OK

"Rewire My Retirement, to me, was a godsend. It helped me develop a different approach to how I start my day, which is now my resolution practice. I now have more grit to be optimistic and I'm developing the energy and the commitment to be who I'm meant to be, instead of who I was."
—Doc Lawrence Nelson, Mclean, VA

"Never ever did I think this would happen to me! I am now enjoying more fulfilling activities than ever before. These tools will help you achieve anything."
—Donna Privette, Columbia, SC

"Through the Rewire My Retirement program, I learned a process that I can repeat for future goals as needed."
—Joyce Miller, Sandy Springs, GA

"The Rewire My Retirement program is an in-depth, enlightening analysis of what it takes to be successful as we advance in years. Cyn is an effective communicator who shares science-based knowledge of how to plan for and go about our days in ways that assure happiness and fulfillment in retirement. I'm so glad I signed up for her program. You will be too."
—Ted Hunter, Seattle, WA

"Cyn's program really is a very helpful system and well laid out for our success."

—Mary Rowe, Portland, OR

"After a prolonged period of feeling really lost and extremely in need of a life direction, I went looking for guidance and found Cyn's Rewire My Retirement program. I immediately started to feel some relief. I felt encouraged by Cyn's dynamic energy. Engaging in her process has been a remarkable journey of discovery for me. I'm so grateful."

—Sally Lomanno, Philadelphia, PA

"For the first time in my life, I'm living in the present. Through Rewire My Retirement, I developed positive daily habits of focusing on myself, my growth, my passions, and my core values. And now my retirement is aligned with it."

—Steve Bram, Charleston, SC

"Cyn Meyer is in my opinion the Retirement Whisperer! Using Cyn's techniques I found that I could repurpose the skills I had developed in my career and use them to build a new vibrant life. More importantly, through her well-researched, detailed, and proscriptive program I was able to get active and begin to heal from the loss of a lifetime. I highly recommend this program to anyone who is getting older and thinking about what comes next. Thanks Cyn!"

—Dan Rutberg, Westchester, NY

FROM **AIMLESS**
TO **AMAZING**

The Rewire Retirement Method

CYN MEYER

PROMINENCE
PUBLISHING

From Aimless to Amazing: The Rewire Retirement Method

Copyright 2024 © by Cyn Meyer
Published by Prominence Publishing

ISBN: 978-1-990830-47-1

This book is dedicated to the all-star students and learn-it-alls who continue to strive to greater and greater heights one micro-step at a time.

For all the readers open-minded enough to embrace modern ways and believe there's more to life than the status quo. May you follow the unique path *you* are meant to take!

CONTENTS

"In the end, it's not the years in your life that count.
It's life in your years."

—Abraham Lincoln

INTRODUCTION

How to Get the Most Out of This Book

INTRODUCTION

This book exists for two reasons:

1. To help you leverage your brain's neuroplasticity and unlock all the possibilities in your most joyful retirement life as the most authentic version of you. In non-coach speak: to achieve a retirement life full of purpose and passion, one that you're meant to live, not one you're conditioned to (by society and your life thus far).

2. To make sure you have a clear plan for implementing your dream life, whether it's through the Rewire My Retirement program or on your own using the steps outlined in this book.

I'm going to be direct and honest with you throughout each chapter. As a practicing certified life coach, I know that sugarcoating does not help.

And I want to help you.

It is important to help you discover your sense of purpose and passion, turning your retirement into the beginning of a big growth journey so that you:

- Understand your new identity and role in retirement

- Are excited about your future possibilities

- Have total clarity on what your ideal life looks like (beyond just finances)

- Have a reliable system in place to turn that into an everyday reality

- Aren't afraid to face the unknowns ahead

- Aren't settling for a sedentary lifestyle, becoming one of the sad statistics

- Smoothly transition into a retirement you love, across all aspects of your life

To do that, I've structured the book as follows.

First, I'll share important details about the lay of the land, including the outdated version of retirement versus the modern way so you don't get stuck in traps stemming from the past. And then I want to give you an honest picture of where you stand today—mentally, physically, financially, personally, and everything in between. You'll learn about my 5 Rings of Retirement framework and will complete several self-assessments to help you pinpoint exactly where you should put your focus next and how best to move forward.

Then I'll share all the steps included in the Rewire Retirement Method, from top to bottom. This is the method I personally and professionally use to help my clients and students achieve an ideal, active, healthy, and engaged retirement lifestyle, full of purpose and passion, where you commit to bettering yourself and growing to greater and greater heights, indefinitely. I'm very excited to share it with you here.

INTRODUCTION

The Rewire Retirement Method is a three-part system that hacks your brain for growth and life satisfaction, specifically during retirement. It leverages the massive power of neuroplasticity, combining neuroscience with specific life coaching tools so you can gain clarity and execute on your most fulfilling retirement life, full of purpose and passion.

In three simple steps, the Rewire Retirement Method is:

1. **Gain Clarity:** First, take inward action to gain clarity on exactly what you want before taking any outward action.

2. **Engage Micro-Steps:** Next, implement outward action in the form of engaging daily micro-steps for one focused piece of your newfound clarity.

3. **Build Momentum:** The third step begins alongside Step #1, where you structure in consistent daily micro-steps from the start and continue through the whole process creating key cumulative benefits.

3-STEP REWIRE RETIREMENT METHOD

Finally, I'll spend some time focusing on quickening your speed to the results you're looking for. All walks of life use the Rewire Retirement Method for success, and I want to share some common brain traps so you can avoid recurrent hang-ups and move through the process faster. I'll show you how to kill procrastination for good, how to leverage the best mindset out there, and how to recognize and overcome hidden blocks that most people fall prey to.

The goal is for you to have a definitive process in place by the time you finish reading this book.

Simply put, the entirety of these pages can be summed up in the following five points:

1. The current stereotypes about aging and retirement contribute to a glaring problem in our culture where older adults are conditioned to strive for much less than they are capable of and to access only a tiny portion of what they truly want out of life.

2. Retirement is not simply about living a life of leisure.

3. There's much more to retirement planning than just financial planning.

4. Retirement is, in fact, the beginning of a big growth journey.

5. You can leverage the power of neuroplasticity to unlock newfound clarity, engage a process that turns your dream life into a reality, and set yourself up for amazing success and growth indefinitely. The method I use is called the Rewire Retirement Method (based on neuroplasticity).

INTRODUCTION

The method you're about to discover radically transforms retirement lives and beyond for the better. It directly applies to people across a vast array of situations and circumstances, and I hope you'll be able to make the connection for yourself too.

Because serving this audience is my personal mission and passion, it's my sincere hope that you learn more than just how to implement the Rewire Retirement Method. I've peppered in cornerstone tools, lessons, and bits of advice that come up as common themes during my many years of guiding clients in private coaching sessions.

Yes, this book is about how to go from aimless to amazing during retirement, and it's also about the magic of neuroplasticity—specifically, how to leverage it to unlock your authenticity from your subconscious brain.

My main hope for you is that you not only gain clarity and unleash it from your brain, but that you adopt a practical process for integrating it, which swiftly leads you to your best, most authentic self and life in your retirement reality.

It's my honor to share with you what I know. Your improved life will only have a positive ripple effect and inspire those around you, multiplying the impact of this movement of older adults striving to be their best. We need more people like you. Thank you for being here!

If you read this book and decide you want help implementing it as quickly as possible, please head over to my fully guided program to activate your success at secondwindmovement.com/rewire.

I'm here to help you on this important journey.

Much love,

Cyn Meyer

PART 1

The Old Way vs. The New Way

"None are so old as those who have outlived enthusiasm."

—Henry David Thoreau

CHAPTER 1

Who Is This Book For?

This book is for anyone who is not afraid to turn stereotypes on their head. Which stereotypes should we avoid? Let's get these big glaring ones out of the way:

Avoid Stereotype #1: Eternal Vacation

If you're not one for falling into the leisurely lifestyle of a stereotypical retiree, then this book is for you (think cruises; senior center activities; traditional volunteering; scrolling social media, Netflix, or news sources; gardening; (grand)parenting; golf and/or pickleball as your peak activities).

Don't get me wrong. Any of the above are very worthwhile, especially if they light you up from the inside out (particularly the grandparenting one). But having these form the **center** of your life's engagement level is something totally different.

In other words, if the sound of an eternal life of leisure doesn't turn you on, and you want *something more* to retirement than just your standard activities and to-do lists, then this book is for you.

I grew up playing violin in retirement homes, and I saw early on what happens with a sedentary lifestyle and how it leads to "waiting out" the end of your life. But when you wait out the rest of your life, things don't get more engaging. Instead, your brain and body turn to *mush*.

Sadly, this stagnant, leisurely lifestyle is a detriment that starts with society's depiction in our culture and media. Which is why it's my personal mission and passion to flip this damaging stereotype on its head.

Avoid Stereotype #2: Old Dog, Old Tricks

This book is for anyone who doesn't want to be *that* old person who becomes less interesting and less relevant as they age, left only to cling on to their past memories, successes, and achievements while repeating the same stories like Groundhog Day circa 1997.

In other words, you're someone who wants to learn, expand your mind, be stimulated, and have intriguing experiences that are new and exciting well into your future. You want a vibrant, relevant life that includes engaging with interesting people, places, and activities—and you want to continue feeling *young*.

I recently conducted my "50 People Over 50" interview series, and 98 percent of the participants stated feeling significantly younger than their true age. The only reason people mentioned feeling older was when they were having bad days due to physical pain (and the single person who identified with an older-than-actual age had a bad post-knee surgery moment).

Knee surgeries and physical ailments aside, this clear trend has a lot to do with the emotional and invisible stuff. Your mental health plays a big role in deciding how you feel as you age, and youthfulness is a proud claim for a lot of people leading happy good lives.

The way to get there is to continue to learn *new* things. Falling into the mindset of "I know myself so well by now" is a trap that keeps you from discovering more about yourself, which is an endless evolution that leads to more authenticity and discovering your true nature.

Please don't cut yourself off from knowing more by being a know-it-all. Instead, be a learn-it-all because *that's* what'll keep your mind and spirit young.

Beyond feeling eternally youthful, this book is also for anyone open-minded and willing to learn new ways to achieve their most fulfilling retirement in modern-day society from a modern retirement life coach who's younger and *(gasp!)* not yet retired.

I'm not writing this book because I want you to replicate my life. In fact, please don't replicate *anyone's* life. (Even if a savvy entrepreneurial sixty-six-year-old retiree wrote this book, the goal isn't for you to replicate the author's life, which is why you will never find the answers you're looking for in what's popular for the demographic or in your loved one's advice, but I digress.)

I'm writing this book to share the steps in my Rewire Retirement Method, which is based on a combo of neuroscience and vital life coaching tools specifically tailored to meet the needs and challenges of those craving a fulfilling retirement.

What I'm teaching you is directly applicable to this specific audience transitioning into retirement. And my program continues to help real-life retirees from all walks of life achieve success.

My main passion and personal mission is to help older adults achieve success, become inspiring models for others around them, and join a movement that shifts our culture to become more successful at aging. As in, more active, healthy, and engaged.

I'm called to and *choose* to serve this audience of older adults because it's important to me.

In case you're interested in fun facts beyond playing music in retirement homes, two significant signposts that also led me to this choice are:

- Both of my grandparents passed away with Alzheimer's, and my dad had brain surgery plus thirty-eight rounds of radiation in 2011. So I took a really deep dive into neuroplasticity to leverage its power for cognitive and mental health.

- While servicing the financial planning industry in a former career, I got to know a clientele of retirees and saw firsthand the "retirement honeymoon period" quickly disappear, where people with big careers and nest eggs fell too fast into a life of stagnancy (there's way more to retirement planning than only financial planning).

Personal bio tidbits aside, my goal is for you to learn a systematic way to achieve a successful retirement. One that guides you inward for newfound clarity and lets neuroplasticity work its magic, brain-hacking your way to your unique ideal lifestyle and growth *indefinitely*.

If you're feeling rudderless, aimless, irrelevant, or lacking energy, then by the end of this book, I want you to *refuse* to accept the infamous rhetoric that says, "It's just part of getting old."

Losing energy is not simply a part of getting old. I'm not denying the normal aging process. I'm talking about specific ways to source your energy and vitality.

All the energy you put into your career and family life floats up while you transition into your retirement role and go through this big identity shift. When that floating energy goes undirected, it typically directs *itself* into a life on autopilot, which typically leads to various forms of anxiety and depression.

My second mission for you is to capture all that pre-retirement energy and convert it into something intentional and *amazing* that will serve you and your best, most authentic life. You're not here to model your parents' or grandparents' retirement. You're here to break generational hand-me-downs that no longer serve you and the greater good.

I don't want you to feel like your best days are behind you. Mark my words: If you follow the growth journey you're meant to take, your heyday is *not* behind you. You have n*ot* peaked. You are fully capable and are built for greater and greater heights.

If you're wondering where your motivation and energy went and why it's been replaced with a heavy dose of procrastination, please read on. There is a trusty (brain hacky) way out. You just need a solid system for gaining clarity and then integrating that dream life into your reality long term.

The single most important takeaway for you out of reading this book is this: your retirement is the *beginning* of a big growth journey.

Modern retirement is not about living a life of only leisure, in the same way that retirement planning is not about only financial planning.

My hope is that you will apply this very systematic, science-based Rewire Retirement Method to unlock so much growth and possibility for yourself that you not only feel deeply satisfied in your own life, but you also inspire success that ripples beyond your own lifetime.

Let's make an impact in a very positive, profound way that's worth modeling for generations to come.

Check-In Exercise

Before we move on, let's first check in with where you currently stand when it comes to your clarity. In the assessment questions below, rate yourself on a scale from 1 to 5 on how accurate or agreeable the statements are.

After rating yourself for each statement, total up your scores and then refer to the Answer Key to understand what your score means.

Strongly Disagree	Disagree	Neutral	Agree	Strongly Agree
1	2	3	4	5

I wake up knowing exactly what to do each day.	
I never get distracted by other projects, requests, or ideas and always stay on task with my plans.	
I know exactly what I want to accomplish in my retirement, and it goes well beyond my bucket list.	
I have much more than a to-do list to accomplish each day. My bigger-picture passion goals are very clear.	
My schedule is perfectly structured and balanced with a good mix of satisfying and fulfilling activities across the board.	
I'm achieving meaningful, fulfilling activities regularly.	
I am a passionate person who is always comfortable morphing into new ideas and plans, even if they're risky.	
I never worry about what to do. I have total clarity.	
I feel very excited about my future and have a solid plan to achieve my goals.	
I never procrastinate and always follow through with my original intentions.	
I have rock-solid daily routines that serve me well. I end each day feeling very satisfied and accomplished.	
I practice mindfulness daily and don't feel right without enhancing my awareness each day.	
TOTAL SCORE	

What Your Score Really Means

*SCORE 0–20: Low Stimulation, Low Growth
(At Risk for Long-Term Rut)*

You're currently in a weak growth mode, and you're a bit under-stimulated. You feel stuck in a retirement rut with only the thoughts spiraling (on repeat) in your head. You're succumbing to the idea that aging is about slowing and settling down into the safety of your comfort zone, and your best days are behind you.

The good news is awareness and clarity will pull you out of any retirement rut. Read this book with an open mind, and consider the idea that you have the power to redesign your life in this brand-new phase. Consider implementing the Rewire Retirement Method from the inside out to discover things about your deepest desires, wishes, dreams, and goals that you didn't give yourself the chance to know beforehand.

*SCORE 21–40: Messy Thinking Is Holding You Back:
Focus Is Needed*

You know that you're not satisfied with the idea of settling down into a sedentary lifestyle; an eternal vacation sounds boring and depressing to you. For long-term satisfaction, you need more energy, motivation, and excitement right now. While relaxation is sometimes a nice pace change, you feel rudderless and "not like yourself."

The good news is you're moderately self-aware and understand that you do have a lot to contribute and experience; it's just about having the right outlet and format. Once you gain clarity and a plan, it's game-on. Using a reliable process for gaining clarity on your new passions and purpose in this life phase will give you the deeply satisfying and exciting experiences you're looking for. Get ready to implement the steps in the Rewire Retirement Method to unlock your possibilities, most of which will be revealed as you continue the process and experience key cumulative benefits.

SCORE 41–60: Systemizing Will Make Life Way Easier (and More Exciting)

You've got ideas, confidence, and energy. You know exactly what you want to accomplish in your retirement life and can even see yourself achieving and experiencing them.

Since you have a good measure of clarity in place, the biggest hurdle for you to overcome is the ping-pong effect, where you bounce around from project to project, or idea to idea. That's where the Rewire Retirement Method comes in—to help you build in a solid system for momentum and consistency. You need both in your daily structure to be successful in the long term. Follow the steps inside this book closely to adopt a successful system and to continue your growth to greater and greater heights.

Key Takeaways

- This book is for anyone who wants to avoid a life of only leisure, which is the stereotypical eternal retirement vacation that leads to an eternal retirement rut.

- This book is for anyone who is willing and who wants to learn something new, avoiding a too-common sedentary lifestyle and fueling a stimulating growth path.

- To live a fulfilling authentic retirement, you need a reliable system in place. You can leverage neuroplasticity to gain clarity and then brain hack the integration process.

- If you don't capture all that energy you invested into your career and family life and then convert it into something intentional (a life full of growth, purpose, meaning, and passion), it'll convert itself into a life lived on autopilot.

- Simply put, your retirement is the *beginning* of a big growth journey.

CHAPTER 2

A Modern Retirement Reality

Let me paint you a picture of what life is like using the Rewire Retirement Method:

It is full of growth. Not the kind of growth that's all about being productive or non stop achieving, either.

This growth feels *intentional* and is full of excitement, passion, and purpose.

It's not like anything you can imagine today as you read this book, because what it does is unlock a new level of clarity. As in new experiences, new passions, and new growth.

For instance, each time someone goes through the full Rewire My Retirement program, they uncover hidden desires that they *truly* want to experience but didn't even know existed (not consciously anyway).

It goes well beyond what you "always imagined retirement would be like." And it goes well beyond what your "old passions that you didn't have time for" have to offer.

A rewired life is so much deeper, richer and more satisfying than what the average retiree allows themselves to experience. Why? Because getting there means you will experience growth, which of course, doesn't come easy. Yet you are meant to evolve, develop, change, and grow at every life stage, and retirement is no different.

In fact, your retirement years are the prime time for BIG growth. Not only because of the wide-open space to detangle the "supposed to-dos" in life, but also because your brain is literally built for it.

Neuroplasticity is your brain's ability to reorganize itself through your environment, behavior, thinking, and emotions. Your brain is "plastic," which means it can modify the strength and efficacy of its synaptic structure, function, or connections. Whether it's internal or external, your nervous system responds to stimuli and can change its synaptic transmission.[1]

This basically means your brain is set up for lifelong learning, adaptation, and evolution.

But not your whole brain, just your modern brain. So let's quickly distinguish between the two.

- **The old brain:** The oldest part of your brain forms your lizard brain (brainstem and cerebellum), which is responsible for going into autopilot and fight-or-flight mode. It has one job: to keep you safe.

- **The modern brain:** The youngest part of your brain is the neocortex and is responsible for language, imagination, and higher thinking skills.

While reserving your energy in survival mode is critical, the issue is that the oldest part of your brain had its glory days full of purpose way back when we needed to survive in the wild (eons before the internet).

The fact that you can create new neural pathways in your brain until the day you die proves that you can use the final third of your lifespan to spiral up, not down. You simply need to access your neocortex and hack your way out of a life lived on autopilot.

In other words, modern (retirement) life requires you to use more of your modern brain.

You Are Wired for Growth

I've had the honor of helping many thousands of older adults since 2018, and this transformation happens time and time again; retirement is the beginning of a big growth journey.

I can say this with confidence: people who rewire their retirement for growth *soar!*

The traditional way to emotionally navigate through retirement is through the 5 Emotional Stages of Retirement. Your main goal is to eventually get out of the rut of Disenchantment (Stage #3) and into Stability (Stage #5).

The old way:

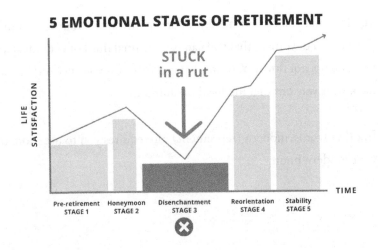

According to a recent US Bureau of Labor Statistics American Time Use Survey, a snapshot trend of what's been happening over a decade is not looking good. Signs are pointing to a growing sedentary lifestyle.

On average, those over age sixty-five spent *more* time watching television, relaxing, and engaging in leisure activities in 2021 than they did a decade ago. And while society pushes financial aspects as *the* top priority for retirement readiness, financial management is nearly last on the list of things retirees spend their time on, averaging merely .06 hours per day compared to 10.74 combined hours of watching television, relaxing, and partaking in leisurely activities.[2]

This current snapshot of an expanded retirement rut where people are less engaged does *not* have to be your reality:

HOW RETIREES SPEND THEIR DAYS

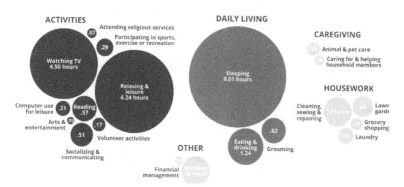

I propose a modern way!

Shorten your time in Disenchantment (Stage #3) and expand well beyond Stability (Stage #5) where you can swell into a massive growth phase that allows you to achieve everything you could dream of experiencing, and more.

The new way:

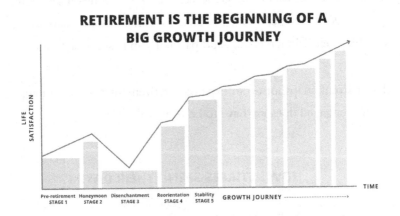

Imagine a life where you unlock your deepest desires, wishes, dreams, and goals in this new life phase. You embody the most authentic version of *you* with that sense of *"Yes!"* and childlike play.

As in, "This is me! This is truly how I want to feel. This is truly who I'm meant to be." And . . .

"I feel alive again!"

The best way people can describe a rewired life is like *feeling* energized, engaged, inspired, motivated, free, fulfilled, satisfied, and balanced. Because the details are more about logistics and format (and can vary as widely as music genres from person to person), the feeling is what's universal.

These ideas about your personal best and your most authentic retirement life will surface in a way that's totally unexpected, especially when you let yourself be wholly open-minded to the process and let the neuroplasticity work its magic.

This isn't an esoteric idyllic life either. It's a science-based methodical way to access the most passionate human parts of you so that you can have it *all*.

Because you *can* have it all—a sense of purpose, meaning, relevance, contribution, *and* responsibilities, duties, to-do lists, completed projects, *and* leisure, relaxation, spontaneity, freedom, *and* a full social life, exciting engagements, and fulfilling relationships.

This all leads to your good health and overall well-being.

Your Path Is Unique, so Let Your Neuroplasticity Guide You

The great news is the Rewire Retirement Method is based on neuroscience. This makes it a very reliable, systematic way to gain clarity and then integrate that clarity into your retirement reality. That's the beauty of it.

When you tap into the power of your neuroplasticity in a very intentional way that goes beyond those well-traveled neural pathways, you create new ways of doing, thinking, and being that are totally aligned and attuned to your authentic self.

In other words, you unlock all these crazy, exciting possibilities and creative ways of connecting your neural brainwaves, which translates into deeply satisfying experiences that you can't even fully imagine at this beginning stage right now.

And again, the details fill in (dramatically) differently for each person. An authentic dream life for you looks entirely different from another person's ideal retirement.

For instance, look to these four all-star students who rewired their retirements.

#1 Chris: Crazy-Cool Career to Riveting Retirement

When I met Chris, he had just retired at age seventy-one from a very successful career as a filmmaker, professor, and author. His life up until retirement was so rewarding, meaningful, busy, and full of *life*.

But like most people, he was trained to only financially prepare for retirement and not so much the lifestyle part.

Which meant that as soon as he crossed that finish line, he felt lost and uncertain and realized that he was in completely unfamiliar territory. Retirement was an entirely new and unnerving experience for him.

He knew he wanted to fill his life with interesting and meaningful activities and projects that he would enjoy (and he had a *ton* of ideas and great intentions), but he was struggling to find the best way to actually make this new life a reality.

Because he was unclear on what exactly to do next, he didn't know where to put his focus. As a result, he got stuck in the rut of Disenchantment (Stage #3).

Then he joined Rewire My Retirement and not only gained clarity; he also found a step-by-step system that guided him through a specific process for living an engaged, active, and healthy lifestyle.

Gaining clarity and engaging micro-steps became his new way of life. And Chris became himself again.

He now uses this exact system and will continue to do so for the rest of his life, beyond the scope of his initial learning of the Rewire Retirement Method.

Chris's so-called retirement life is so robust, rewarding, and impressive that it's a misnomer to call this period of his life his "retirement" (but that's what this movement is all about: redefining the traditional stereotype).

A very brief highlight of Chris's latest accomplishments and immediate plans include:

- Leaving a legacy and writing six books on topics that he's passionate about

- Prioritizing his relationship with his wife, and enjoying joint activities like dancing, tennis, and traveling

- Nurturing his role as father and grandfather to his three daughters and grandchildren

- Exercising vigorously for an hour each day

- Giving back to the community by continuing to provide education, workshops, and speaking gigs

- Serving on local boards for causes that he believes in

- Taking piano lessons and teaching his grandchildren how to play

- Volunteering at local hospice locations

The list goes on, and now he has an abundance of growth experiences to carry out in a very reliable way. He can count on living out his ideal retirement lifestyle over the long term.

"Cyn is a gifted coach and an expert on everything to do with aging and retirement.

I highly recommend her program to anyone interested in making sure their final decades are the best years of their lives, brimming with fun, engagement, love, companionship, caring, creativity, good health, and giving. I love Cyn's emphasis on growth, giving back, health, community, achieving goals, micro-steps, and living an engaged, active lifestyle. "

—Chris Palmer

#2 Paulett: Pipe-Dreamer to Passion-Pursuer

Paulett is someone who is a super helper.

Throughout her career as a teacher, and after decades of raising her daughter alongside her husband, she found herself in retirement full of ambitious ideas and energy. Yet so many of her great ideas remained stuck in her head, and she didn't know what next steps to take for a vibrant, fulfilling lifestyle once again.

She had no concrete way to channel all those ideas and all that energy, so she identified as a dreamer and not a doer.

Admittedly, she wasn't sure about the Rewire Retirement Method at first, but boy did she soar afterward.

Paulett went from a pipe-dreamer to a passion-project pursuer.

All she needed was a bit of clarity and the right tools to keep her consistently on track with her most meaningful, exciting, and *fun* retirement goals.

Today, Paulett enjoys activities like:

- Teaching chair yoga every week

- Hosting online yoga lessons from her home studio

- Spending weekends at her new beach house

- Attending a virtual book club that she started during the pandemic

- Walking weekly with her walking buddies

- Enjoying improved relationships with her husband and family members

- Attending local events with a mix of new and old friends

- Continuing her ambition to explore more creative outlets

And that's just the tip of what she's accomplished after learning the Rewire Retirement Method.

The best part?

This kind of personal growth can only enhance your relationships. It's a side effect that happens 100 percent of the time you focus on yourself and do the inner work.

The tools and coaching Paulett gained from rewiring her life have given her more self-confidence, the ability to trust herself, and a beautiful reconnection with her authenticity, which *drastically* improved her marriage and relationship with her daughter.

These accomplishments are simply side effects of coming into your own and being wholly responsible for turning your dreams into your reality. *You* get to own that work, and it feels *good*.

"If you look back and see all the things I've done, it's really amazing.

I was a person who would dream of all these things, but the action was keeping me from doing it. I wasn't sure at first, but once I got into the program, I was really pleased with the whole experience.

I'm more self-confident, calm, consistent, and a more positive person. I've even improved my relationship with my husband. I loved it."
—Paulett Amburn

#3 Steve: From Murky to Magnificent

Steve is a wonderful family man with a blessed, robust life who just needed some clarity and help with the next steps as he dove deeper into his so-called "retired life."

Two years ago, he tiptoed his way into the Rewire My Retirement program.

I say *tiptoe* because, like most people, he was not sure about joining at first.

After digging into the Rewire Retirement Method, he immediately felt a profound "when the student is ready, the teacher shows up" energy.

He started practicing mindfulness in a way that he never had before.

He found a deep sense of peace and clarity that helped him take consistent action—the kind of action that leads you to fulfilling and meaningful accomplishments.

Needless to say, he became a dream student who hit the ground running and has experienced so much success. Yes, it's true. Being a hard worker who takes a leap of faith has a lot to do with someone's success.

But another huge factor that I keep hearing about is . . . *timing.*

Talk about timing for Steve. Not that he (or anyone) can predict when hardship arrives, but it's a very good thing Steve took that leap of faith and joined the program when he did.

He learned some key tools that were instrumental in helping him through some pretty rough times right after enrolling, such as:

- Falling (twice!) on a rocky slope while hiking on a camping trip with his two grandsons

- Becoming very ill, to the point of being bedridden for months

- Welcoming his teenage granddaughter into his home as a long-term shelter from traumatic familial issues

- Experiencing two mini strokes that zapped his energy for weeks

Fast forward to today. Steve is stronger than ever. Truly.

Steve is hiking nearby foothills like a maniac (he reported doing 10,000 steps a week) and leading daily walks with neighbors...

Oh! He successfully climbed Mt. Lassen again for his seventieth birthday. Wow!

It is truly inspiring when someone like Steve applies the tools from Rewire My Retirement while enduring hardships along the way. He didn't use them as an excuse to stop, and he literally became unstoppable.

Steve has a rock-solid resilience and equanimity for everything physically and emotionally rigorous.

If you're on the fence about the Rewire Retirement Method, you're not alone. In fact, I'd say most of the people who enroll in the fully guided program are skeptical at first. I don't blame them. There's an overload of empty marketing promises out there that we've all been exposed to.

Yet there *is* something about taking a leap of faith at the right time.

"I can see how this is going to have a huge impact on the rest of my life.

The powerful tools I learned in the program helped me get through life's challenges. You can pretty well get through everything if you use the tools. They're now a part of my everyday life."

—Steve Gardner

#4 Sue: Total Fear to Total Clarity

I also want to share a quick snippet about Sue, an energetic, creative, get-things-done kind of woman who already had her (more than) fair share of ambitious projects she was involved in.

Even as a pre-retiree, she had her hands in so many pots outside of work, including dancing, storytelling, music, and writing a memoir.

Yet even with varied interests, connections, and project ideas, Sue had anxiety and fear about entering retirement. So much so that she kept putting it off. She even had a resignation letter written and ready to go, but she just couldn't pull the trigger and kept pushing her retirement date back.

Her main issue? Her retirement fear was just too strong, and the lack of clarity started to paralyze her projects even outside of work.

As with most of her personal projects, while writing her book she came to a roadblock about 75 percent of the way through. The deeper issue? She lacked clarity:

- Clarity on her post-career pathway and how it would all play out

- Clarity on how she would continue to fulfill her purpose

- Clarity on her identity in this new phase

To say the least, this lack of clarity impacted the completion of her book *and* her retirement readiness.

The good news is she learned the Rewire Retirement Method and first gained clarity on what she wanted to pursue and in what order she wanted to prioritize it. Then she became clear on how to both set and achieve her personal deadlines.

With this clarity came a very powerful behavior change. Sue not only surpassed her 75 percent completion mark (as of this writing, her book is already pre-launched), but she also unlocked *two* more books from inside her.

More importantly, she slowly shed her fear of retiring. It's clear there's a lot more creativity, storytelling, dancing, traveling, and impact-making in Sue's future. And this is only the beginning!

After working with so many amazing people transitioning into retirement, I have found that the "unknown" of retirement and having a wide-open schedule to pursue *any* activity can be overwhelming to the point of paralysis. And, of course, there's always pesky procrastination.

The "freedom" of retirement tends to not feel "free" for very long; instead, it feels *frightening*. It's the kind of fear that stops you smack dab in the middle of your tracks.

Once you gain clarity, though, the foundation for true fulfillment is secured. Your next job is to then continue the oh-so-reliable "consistent micro-stepping" rhythm with the outward action. And after consistent micro-stepping is rewired into your system, the magic is unleashed.

I'm a firm believer that *you* have unique gifts to share with the world to make it a better place. Here's to unleashing your magic and to sharing *your* unique gifts. They are much-needed.

"Cyn's program has given me the courage to move forward in this new life of retirement.

What makes the process effective for me is that it's broken down into bits and pieces and mini-habits. And those mini-habits are built upon other mini-habits. I'm a true believer in incremental change and incremental improvement. Now I have a nice basis for why I will retire. "

—Sue Camaione

Rewiring Works for All Walks of Life

When I say rewiring works for all walks of life, this system literally applies to everyone of all ages. It doesn't matter who you are or how old you are; you can use the Rewire Retirement Method to unlock a very clear purpose and reason and then integrate that into your real life.

It doesn't matter if I'm in my forties or eighties. I use this system to rewire my own life and to unlock my most fulfilling, satisfying, and enjoyable life. I even use it with my kids. But I specifically tailor it to help older adults because I deeply care about this audience.

Yes, while it's my personal calling to be a life coach for older adults, *your results* are the amazing things that our society *needs* to see you do because it will enhance everyone around you. This is how we create that cornerstone ripple effect, where people around you get to model this new rewired way of being in this modern environment of the modern retirement era.

So thank you for taking on your own personal journey to do this important work.

Key Takeaways

- The "old way" of retirement relies heavily on your lizard brain to call the shots. This is the oldest part of your brain that keeps you safely inside your comfort zone. Sadly, this often means being stuck in a traditional retirement rut, namely Disenchantment (Stage #3).

- The "new way" of retirement relies more on your neocortex, the youngest part of your brain in touch with growth and striving for your dream life, goals, wishes, and desires.

- You are wired for growth; you just need a (modern) system for accessing this conscious part of your brain to gain clarity, intentional growth, and new, fulfilling experiences.

- The Rewire Retirement Method works for all types of people across all kinds of preferences, backgrounds, histories, lifestyles, situations, and circumstances. Gaining clarity and executing on your dreams is merely an inward journey and individual brain game.

CHAPTER 3

The Top 3 Challenges Retirees Face

These top three challenges that retirees face can be solved with the Rewire Retirement Method. I'm sharing these with you so that you can:

- Proactively avoid and/or shorten your time in Stage #3 of Disenchantment (aka the retirement rut)

- Understand the ins and outs of the Rewire Retirement Method and use them in the most focused, effective, quick, and consistent way in your daily life

Challenge #1: Lack of Purpose

I have found the number one challenge people face when transitioning into retirement is losing their sense of purpose. This is directly related to a major shift in your role and identity and how you contribute.

A purposeless life is a big source of anxiety for people, especially if you're used to a big career with lots of accolades, responsibilities, and achievements. Even if retirement is something you've looked forward to for years, crossing that finish line can feel like losing a part of yourself. So much so that it can resemble an identity crisis.

This makes sense if you think back to the number of times you've been asked, "What do you do?" Only to answer with your job title. Or the common small talk about your profession immediately after introducing yourself to someone new.

Your professional identity is a big deal, and this familiar terrain has been with you for decades.

Let me offer you a reframe: Retirement doesn't erase your professional identity; it simply diversifies it. In fact, according to research on personal identity after retirement, it remains a significant part of how you see yourself.[1] So it's definitely not worth shaming yourself if you don't shake it or replace it.

The study also found that retirement doesn't limit self-description. In fact, quite the opposite. Retirees rate more domains as important for self-description than the non-retirees. Which means with retirement comes a greater diversity in identity.

Put another way, you're not just retired; that's merely your employment status. Instead, you're expanding and diversifying your self-identify post-retirement, whether it's sprinkling in titles like *artist, gardener, world explorer, athlete, author, grandparent,* or *small business owner.*

The Rewire Retirement Method addresses this number one issue head-on by directly probing your brain for specific answers about your sense of purpose. You'll find most of these answers inside the "Giving Back" category of the 5 Rings of Retirement framework.

More on the 5 Rings of Retirement in the next chapter, but basically it's critical to explore different ways that helping others naturally lights you up. And I don't mean traditional forms of volunteering— far from it.

The way that you share your unique gifts, and the style and format that doing so takes on, is going to be vastly different (and eclectic) for every retiree.

Challenge #2: Lack of Structure

Going from a tight, rigid structure to a totally open structure is like going from 60 to 0 miles per hour in a heartbeat, *even if you have too much on your plate.*

THE TOP 3 CHALLENGES RETIREES FACE

There are *so* many layers of "transitioning" happening all at once when you retire. To name a few:

- Identity shift

- Sense of purpose shift

- Habit shock: learning to spend down your savings instead of socking it away

- Losing the biggest, most convenient daily social interaction that your job provided

It doesn't matter if any of these are positive or negative; they've been habitually integrated into your daily life. And your body and brain are pretty hooked into a repetitive pattern.

It's no wonder that, when faced with an open schedule and no clarity in a brand new-life phase, your system doesn't know what to do with all this new freedom, so it clings on to the habits already ingrained.

The items on your to-do list and your bucket list lack urgency and priority, and suddenly your sense of accomplishment and pride get quickly replaced with procrastination and lack of motivation. At this point, instead of feeling good, you feel *guilty*.

For people who are extra conditioned to go-go-go, they find themselves ping-ponging from one thing to the next, not making deep progress in any one area, and the days quickly get away from them.

The reason for this is that your good old limbic system is overactive, keeping you safely in your comfort zone and allowing your emotions to dictate your days. This results in you waiting to feel like doing something. Of course, without structure, that motivation never comes.

To have success and fulfillment, retirement structure is crucial. The Rewire Retirement Method teaches you to layer in specific, intentional, daily micro-steps so you're not overwhelmed by decision-fatigue, stewing in procrastination, or relying on your emotions to call the shots.

Challenge #3: Fear of the Unknown

On the topic of procrastination and lack of motivation, it goes without saying that fears in general do their fair share of keeping you stuck in analysis paralysis. I hear a lot about people "getting in their own way" by overthinking choices, hypotheticals, and steps.

At the root of being "aimless" and "rudderless" in retirement is a pesky fear of the unknown.

That type of thinking can quickly spiral into a sad and scary momentum all on its own. What started as a simple anxiety about what to do for the day swells into a monstrous fear about existentialism, and you find yourself pondering if and how you'll make the most of your remaining days.

When that happens, no single action is clear because you're clouded by the dooming fear storm. And then procrastination, analysis paralysis, and mindless tasking take over and you wait for a better or more urgent time to address what's happening beneath the surface.

The main details our society teaches us to tackle are financially based. But you know financial planning isn't the only crucial topic for a successful retirement. This isn't the real picture, where you have an iceberg on top showing only Financial Planning and nothing below:

The old way:

WHAT'S BELOW THE RETIREMENT SURFACE?

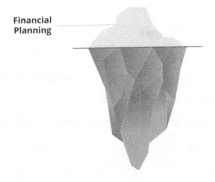

Financial
Planning

This limited view keeps all the meaningful (equally as important) aspects of life invisible; hence, your fear of the unknown exists because you can't clearly put your finger on what I call the "subtle void that hums and grows in the background."

What's really below the retirement surface? Here's a more accurate look at what needs your attention:

The new way:

WHAT'S BELOW THE RETIREMENT SURFACE?

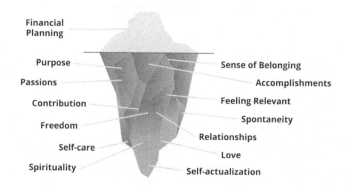

You have the traditional Financial Planning topic on top, and below the surface are massively important factors that remain invisible, such as purpose, passions, contribution, freedom, self-care, spirituality, sense of belonging, accomplishments, feeling relevant, spontaneity, relationships, love, and self-actualization.

Just because it's invisible to the naked eye doesn't mean it's not an enormous factor in your overall life satisfaction, happiness, and well-being.

The Rewire Retirement Method is used in conjunction with a very simple 5 Rings of Retirement framework as its main subject matter. I'm about to share with you the 5 Rings of Retirement framework so you can sidestep a negative thought spiral caused by too many options.

In other words, these five core categories are the topics injected into your daily process.

Please know that there is no perfect time to take care of these areas of your life. There is no perfect setup for giving yourself access to the best life possible. And I don't have to tell you that time is of the essence or that invincibility doesn't last forever.

Just because it's not tangible doesn't mean there's no sense of urgency, and not because you're going to die soon, but because you could be enjoying *now* so much more.

Let's head into a check-in exercise for each of these three challenges and then go right into the 5 Rings of Retirement.

Check-In Exercise

Before we move on, let's first check in with where you currently stand when it comes to the top challenges retirees face and your specific situation. In the assessment questions below, rate yourself on a scale from 1 to 5 on how accurate or agreeable the statements are.

After rating yourself for each statement, total up your scores and then refer to the Answer Key to understand what your score means.

Strongly Disagree	Disagree	Neutral	Agree	Strongly Agree
1	2	3	4	5

I wake up knowing exactly what to do each day.	
I never get distracted by other projects, requests, or ideas and always stay on task with my plans.	
I know exactly what I want to accomplish in my retirement, and it goes well beyond my bucket list.	
I have much more than a to-do list to accomplish each day. My bigger-picture passion goals are very clear.	
My schedule is perfectly structured and balanced with a good mix of satisfying and fulfilling activities across the board.	
I'm achieving meaningful, fulfilling activities regularly.	
I am a passionate person who is always comfortable morphing into new ideas and plans, even if they're risky.	
I never worry about what to do. I have total clarity.	
I feel very excited about my future and have a solid plan to achieve my goals.	
I never procrastinate and always follow through with my original intentions.	
I have rock-solid daily routines that serve me well. I end each day feeling very satisfied and accomplished.	
I practice mindfulness daily and don't feel right without enhancing my awareness each day.	
TOTAL SCORE	

What Your Score Really Means

SCORE 0–16: Depleted, Deep in a Retirement Rut

Your overall energy is low, and the ideas you once had for your retirement life seem like a far-off, unattainable pipe dream. You find yourself struggling to get things done like you used to, and you're lacking motivation and passion.

Real talk: You *can* change the trajectory of your life. Unlike society's depiction of aging, you don't have to sit around and wait for things to happen to you. That's a trap. You just need to focus on the areas that are in your control (aka the brain patterns that are malleable and ready for plasticity), which means gaining clarity and then systemizing a way to integrate that clarity. The Rewire Retirement Method can do that for you. Open up to the process and commit to a consistent effort.

SCORE 17–33: Just Need More Juice. Time to Fine-Tune

While you may be somewhat comfortable, you're stuck in a rut and don't get as excited about accomplishing and achieving like you used to. You find yourself wondering, *What's next?* Sometimes you even wonder, *What for?*

The good news is you're just a few tweaks away from activating your dream retirement life. You need only more clarity and consistency to turn those dreamy ideas into a reality. Your best days are not behind you, so please be intentional in following the steps of the Rewire

Retirement Method. This is how you bust through any classic retirement fears and direct your precious energy toward specific places that will boost your life satisfaction.

SCORE 34–50: You're Ready to Go-Go-Grow!

It's time to accelerate your growth and challenge yourself to greater heights. Your next step is to uncover more untapped potential and consider new formats and ways to generate life satisfaction.

With a great experience under your belt so far, it's important to set your future up for more decades of upward trajectory so you don't plateau and settle for stagnancy. Even the greatest achievers can plateau at the top, which leaves them at risk for declining mentally and emotionally. After all, you're designed to continually evolve and develop, which creates room for different kinds of growth and opens you up to new topics of learning. These things are key to your long-term success.

Key Takeaways

There are three top challenges that retirees face as they transition into this important life phase.

- **Top Challenge #1: Lack of Purpose:** Society places so much emphasis on associating your identity with your career or family role that when it comes to retirement, it can send you into an identity crisis, leaving you with a sense of purposelessness.

- **Good News:** You can rewire your brain to gain clarity on your new purpose and role in retirement.

- **Top Challenge #2: Lack of Structure:** Going from a bustling career and family schedule to a wide-open retirement calendar can stop you in your tracks. To achieve everything you want, a post-career structure is equally important to a pre-retirement one.

- **Good News:** You can leverage neuroplasticity to structure intentional habits and behaviors, and build positive momentum for your new way of life.

- **Top Challenge #3: Fear of the Unknown:** Traditionally, we're taught to only prepare financially for retirement. We are not expected or trained to pay attention to the other vital topics. Fearing the confusion and unknowns below the retirement surface can keep you stuck in a rut. And because these challenges are dominantly invisible, the unfortunate trend is to be in denial of, deprioritize, or postpone addressing these important factors that make up your dream retirement life.

  Good News: The 5 Rings of Retirement framework can bring clarity to the chaos and directly address the confusing, subtle void that hums and grows in the background.

CHAPTER 4

The 5 Rings of Retirement

To achieve a fulfilling, satisfying retirement life full of passion and purpose, one where you feel energized and alive again, you need to dig into specific topics and questions inside the 5 Rings of Retirement framework.

As you know, the big, gaping hole in our society is that we're taught to *only* financially prepare for retirement and not prepare so much the other stuff. Which is why "Finance" is only one of the core categories in the 5 Rings of Retirement, with the sole purpose of supporting the other four more meaningful, rich, colorful aspects of your life.

Inside my fully guided Rewire My Retirement program, I walk you through a daily brain-probe and deep dive into each of the 5 Rings. For now, let's head into the nuances of each core area.

Ring #1: Growth

I've been touting the topic of growth a lot, and it's worth getting granular here. Growth includes so many things under the umbrella of "mental stimulation," and it varies across preferences: lifelong learning, new experiences, challenges, adventures, and meaningful work.

In the same way that your skin cells, gut microbiome, and nails continue to grow and regenerate, your brain cells and *your growth experiences* do the same. And for a lot of people, they experience great spiritual growth.

Regardless of your personal preferences, if you allow yourself to get lazy and don't challenge yourself to learn new things, overcome new challenges, collect growth experiences, or develop as a person, then your mind and body are likely to decline much more quickly.

In fact, for older adults, engaging in mentally challenging activities can reduce your risk of Alzheimer's by 2.5 times.[1]

What's more, if you're an older adult learning multiple new skills simultaneously, your cognitive ability will improve to levels similar to that of a thirty-year-old.[2]

Here's the gist: Exercise your brain like you would any other muscle in your body. Your cognitive health tightly follows the "use it or lose it" principle.

By following the 5 Rings of Retirement framework, you'll keep tabs on your growth level. And you'll also integrate consistent growth into your life long term.

Ring #2: Community

Whether you're an introvert or extrovert, your relationships and social life are fundamentally a significant part of your happiness, health, and overall wellness. Paying close attention to your relationships and social engagements is massively important, which means your spouse, family, friends, neighbors, acquaintances, coworkers, classmates, and everyone in between.

There's such a strong correlation between social interaction and your health, especially among retirees because it becomes less convenient to meet new people. Suddenly, the daily interactions you have with coworkers is halted, so you need to intentionally replace that form of socialization with some other kind. Being actively involved in your community—whether it's engaging with your neighbor or the community at large—is one way to keep you from feeling isolated and lonely.

As for the research, there have been so many studies conducted that reveal being social and involved in your community is good for your health:

- Increases longevity: engaging in social friendship and social-cultural activities is linked to lower mortality rates in seniors.[3]

- Improves cardiovascular health: a study by Fadia T Shaya and the research team found that social networks help control hypertension.[4]

- Loneliness puts you at a 59 percent greater risk of mental and physical decline.[5]

- Social isolation is associated with nearly 27 percent increased risk of dementia.[6]

It's worth noting that as you grow older, the influence of your friends on your health and overall well-being becomes greater and greater, surpassing even that of your family.[7]

To say the least, this area of your life is a foundational ingredient for a robust retirement. My framework keeps this top of mind, and the Rewire Retirement Method helps you probe this area to gain clarity.

Ring #3: Health

Paying attention to how your everyday life impacts not only your physical health but also your mental, emotional, and brain health is critical. We all know diet and exercise are the way to prioritize your health. Also keep in mind that the lifestyle choices you make, including the invisible cognitive exercising, is a big part of that.

To give you an idea of the health-related norms, so you can strive for (much) better than average, check these out:

- A third of older adults die with dementia, affecting more than breast and prostate cancer combined.[8]

- Every eleven seconds, an older adult is treated in the emergency room for a fall.[9]

- Adults lose muscle mass at a rate as high as 3 to 8 percent per decade after the age of thirty.[10]

- At least 10 percent of the older population doesn't meet the required micronutrient standards.[11]

- According to the CDC, almost a third of adults over the age of fifty don't engage in any physical activity.[12]

- Most pre-retirees claim they'll eat healthier and get more exercise during retirement (48 percent), yet retirement reality looks more like wishful thinking.[13]

I don't need to toss in a PSA here. You know your health is an important category. Just remember to hone in on the invisible health factors too, such as mental health and lifestyle choices. Fortunately, the other Rings of Retirement will cross over and also play a helpful role in your overall health and well-being.

Ring #4: Giving Back

The Giving Back ring is where you'll find your sense of purpose. In fact, studies show that volunteering significantly helps older adults regain a sense of purpose and identity.[14]

I want to point out that volunteering is often more satisfying when it's done through nontraditional forms of giving back. In fact, most people get quickly burned out on traditional forms of volunteering (which is why following the Rewire Retirement Method of going inward to gain clarity is so powerful).

There is also a significant amount of research that says giving back is good for your health and your well-being overall, including these few highlights:

Simple things like giving practical help to your family or friends and neighbors lowers your risk of dying.[15]

- Older-adult volunteers reported strengthened levels of self-esteem and self-confidence.[16]

- A dose of oxytocin hormone gets released every time you conduct an act of kindness, which can also be cardioprotective.[17]

Whether it's formal or informal—volunteering, caregiving, publishing something creative and putting it out into the world, gifting some sort of legacy, or explaining your wisdom—the 5 Rings of Retirement fills your innate desire to help others and make an impact.

Ring #5: Finance

While it's not everything, your financial well-being does play a huge factor in your overall stress and wellness levels. If you have financial peace of mind, and the money part of your life is comfortably nestled inside a controlled budget, you can use your finances to fuel your satisfaction in the other 4 Rings of Retirement.

Unfortunately, over 50 percent of Americans fear they'll outlive their retirement savings.[18] Whether that's due to the awkward stage of relearning how to only spend down money (versus only saving it), or the daunting statistic that says the average American will need at least $1.1 million to retire comfortably, gaining clarity in this Finance ring is necessary and foundational.[19]

Use the 5 Rings of Retirement Framework

There's a lot of crossover that can happen between the 5 Rings of Retirement, but these main areas serve as a foundation to balance your life.

Let me repeat: Each person is unique. Not only will you prioritize these rings differently from your next-door neighbor, sister, or spouse, but what you see as a level 2 will perhaps be someone else's level 5.

For example, if someone's top priority and main focus in life is physical health and they're not experiencing any health scares, they may see a level 5 as being fit enough to climb mountains and compete in marathons. Whereas a level 5 for someone who prioritizes the Community ring and relationships over the Health ring may see a level 5 in Health as having diabetes and their A1C counts under control, and/or fitting into the same outfit they wore on their wedding day.

There's no right or wrong preference. And there's no better way to understand the framework than to simply use it in real time. Let's do an assessment.

Check-In Exercise

Before we move on, let's first check in with where you currently stand when it comes to the 5 Rings of Retirement and your energy level. In the assessment questions below, rate yourself on a scale from 1 to 5 on how accurate or agreeable the statements are.

After rating yourself for each statement, total up your scores and then refer to the Answer Key to understand what your score means.

Strongly Disagree	Disagree	Neutral	Agree	Strongly Agree
1	2	3	4	5

I am always challenging myself to learn something new and exciting.	
I am intellectually stimulated and do not feel worried about my cognitive health.	
I am intellectually stimulated and do not feel worried about my cognitive health.	
I have great relationships in my life, and I am constantly deepening my connections with people.	
I prioritize my physical health and well-being and have a strong health regimen in place.	
I feel very strong and confident about my physical and mental health. I don't worry about being able to do things in the future.	
When it comes to volunteering, I'm never burned out. I constantly find new ways of helping others and plan to volunteer my whole life.	

I am currently thriving because I am contributing, helping others, and sharing my unique gifts.	
I am very confident about my financial health and feel secure about not outliving my money.	
Even though I've been growing my wealth for decades, I am very comfortable only spending down my money and have a clear budget and plan.	
TOTAL SCORE	

What Your Score Really Means

SCORE 0–16: Fears Have a Stronghold. You Need More Passion and Purpose

You have anxiety and fear about the future and sadness about the past. Maybe you are missing the life you once had or wishing things could be different. Either way, you're missing passion and purpose and dread a life that feels like eternal disenchantment.

There's a lot of conditioning wired into your thought patterns, which means it's time for a refreshing reboot. And the good news is following the Rewire Retirement Method will give you a process for rerouting from those brain traps driven by fear. To get out of your rut, please be open-minded about transforming your life. Let yourself embrace change, growth, and lifelong learning.

SCORE 17–33: You Need to Break Out of Old Patterns

While you're familiar with the go-go, high-achieving life, the passions that used to excite you no longer do. Falling into a sadness about missing the "good ole days" is a routine your mind easily slips into. Your daily structure is wide open, but you're locked in by fears of the unknown, which puts you at risk for procrastinating on things you need to do and activities you may even enjoy.

Please follow the inward journey specifically prompted by the Rewire Retirement Method. Your definition of retirement success looks completely different from the next person, so now is the time to stop comparing yourself to others and to gain clarity from within. The rest is a brain game of systemizing your outward action plan.

SCORE 34–50: Time for High-Performance Help. Secure Your Future Satisfaction

You are now at a point where your next big task is to dream bigger. It's about future pacing in a new way that will bring you greater levels of life satisfaction, purpose, passion, and meaning well into the next decades.

For you, the next obstacle is to leverage your growth for long-term life satisfaction. Not only should you avoid falling into a big slump; you should also experience satisfaction and make an impact for years that ripples even beyond your lifetime. The way to do that is to systemize your next-level growth so you continue to learn, discover, evolve, and strive for excellence. You are not meant to go stale.

Key Takeaways

The 5 Rings of Retirement is a simple framework that you can use to gauge your life as a snapshot to pinpoint where you need to focus your attention *now*. Your energy level in each ring will ebb and flow over time. It's simply a matter of capturing your current situation so you can easily see what needs your attention for your current season (be it a week, month, or year).

- **Retirement Ring #1—Growth:** lifelong learning, new experiences, meaningful work, brain plasticity, and embracing challenges

- **Retirement Ring #2—Community:** relationships, friendships, social life, and engagement in your community

- **Retirement Ring #3—Health:** diet, exercise, longevity, energy levels, cognitive health, physical health, and mental and emotional health

- **Retirement Ring #4—Giving Back:** sense of purpose, sharing your unique gifts, legacy, volunteering, gifting, helping others, and contribution

- **Retirement Ring #5—Finance:** financial security, not outliving your money, budgeting, legacy, and estate planning

CHAPTER 5

The #1 Problem with Rewiring

The number one problem with rewiring is that *unintentional rewiring* can happen on its own. Put another way, the number one problem with neuroplasticity is knowing about neuroplasticity and *yet not doing anything to work it in your favor.*

Basically, you run the risk of the "rewiring" taking on a life of its own, where you're not the one in the driver's seat. While it's comforting to know that you can:

- create new neural pathways in your brain until the day you die, and

- form new habits, make changes, and live the life you truly want at any given point

Unfortunately, for some people, that's a dangerous piece of information because they now have a reason to *wait (dun, dun, dun),* thinking, *I can always take care of this [rewiring] later.*

When it comes to *procrastinating* on **planning** your ideal retirement, the common phrases I hear from people are:

- *"I have it better than so many others."*

- *"I should just be grateful for what I have."*

- *"I'm not deeply depressed or anxious."*

- *"I'm getting by just fine."*

Yes, those are all very true. And your lizard brain's job, after all, is to keep you safe in your comfort zone to reserve your energy.

But as you know, we're talking about tapping your modern brain for a deeper sense of life satisfaction where you can really let yourself dream big. You know, get more out of life without letting all the possibilities fall by the wayside. (Sidenote: there's also a deeper sense of real gratitude that comes with it.)

The caveat with rewiring is that when you leave your current brain pathway "as is," it rewires itself into the mediocre stereotypical lifestyle. (Or worse, it rewires itself into depression and anxiety.) And for classic retirees, this is where they *only* concern themselves with the financial aspect of retirement instead of the other important areas of life. As in, they don't go deep into *all* 5 Rings of Retirement to find clarity.

There's more to life than money, right? But for some reason, when it comes to retirement planning, the typical retiree allows all the other (more meaningful) subjects to get deprioritized and defaulted to status-quo-ho-hum-business-as-usual survival mode, which in your brain means that you *procrastinate* on creating the life you truly want, leading to a bigger issue.

Danger: It Wires in the Old Way, Deeper and Deeper

The conditioned thought patterns and behaviors that no longer serve you get further cemented into your "way of being." As a result, getting unstuck becomes more difficult the longer you leave neuroplasticity up to its own devices.

You may also find yourself walking into this retirement phase "winging it," which means your subconscious pathways (that are very well-paved and well-traveled) become more deeply entrenched, leaving little room for new growth and new wiring.

More specifically, you may fall into the trap of the old way.

According to Dr. Ken Dychtwald's longevity perspective, the old way of looking at your life span is in three clean stages:

- **Education:** from infancy to adolescence

- **Work and Family:** mid-life period from age twenty to sixty

- **Leisure:** retirement age to end of life[1]

The old way:

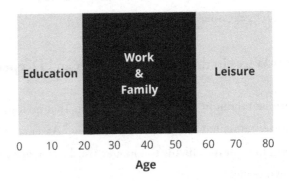

One of the biggest disservices that our current stereotype of "retirement" does for this older generation is instilling the idea that it's time to settle down and live a life of only leisure.

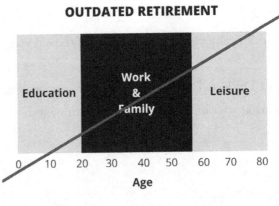

The new way of looking at it is more interspersed between all three stages of education, work and family, and leisure, especially with the injection of technology and the internet (let alone the impact of AI comin' in hot). *Interspersed* is clearly the more keen way to both survive *and* thrive in modern-day retirement.

The new way:

MODERN RETIREMENT

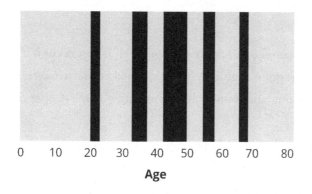

For the high-achievers who have been used to go-go-go careers, lots of accolades, and bustling family lifestyles, retiree stereotypes are *not* for them.

Another very common theme among successful careerists who are used to being at the top of their game is when asked about what they'd replace the stereotypical retirement lifestyle with, they come up blank. They know what they *don't* want (and what they despise), yet they can't see what they *do* want.

Of course, this makes sense. These people have been so busy achieving and providing for external motivations (be it money or other rewards), the intrinsic passions and purpose haven't been prodded nor nurtured in a while.

My absolute favorite thing about the Rewire Retirement Method is you get to leverage neuroplasticity and systematically dispel the myths and stereotypes out there that keep you totally locked in and limited to what you're supposed to experience in so-called "retirement."

For most people, a life of leisure-only is not gonna cut it. A daily to-do list isn't gonna cut it. And heck, a bucket list isn't even gonna cut it. I'm talking about unleashing something much deeper than that.

Put another way, the things that you came to Earth to experience in this lifetime are uniquely wondrous and adventurous and rich. And more often than not, some of the most *amazing* experiences are to be unlocked during retirement.

This makes sense because it really is the beginning of a big growth journey. This is the time when you get to unravel the conditioning that society has entangled into your life and finally make it your own without the intense pressure of your peak career and family life.

To do this, though, you need to proactively convert all that active energy, focus, and effort into something intentional using the power of neuroplasticity . . . or you will lose it.

THE REWIRE RETIREMENT METHOD

Use it or lose it.

According to research, if a brain cell isn't used to learning something new and communicating with the cell next door, that brain cell loses its function and dies off.[2]

And according to Cleveland Clinic's Healthy Brains, your brain "processes 70,000 thoughts each day using 100 billion neurons that connect at more than 500 trillion points through synapses that travel 300 miles per hour."[3]

If you're consciously thinking at the pace of anywhere near the speed of reading this book, then you likely have 70,000 thoughts per day. Most of them are done on autopilot with the subconscious part of your brain and are the same exact thoughts from yesterday's pattern.

Your lizard brain (very quickly) takes over and repeatedly rewires the impulsive old thought patterns, habits, and decisions, leaving you in an indefinite state of procrastination (not to mention lack of motivation, clarity, and energy). As a result, you are left with a stereotypical sedentary lifestyle.

That's not your story though. You know there's something bigger, juicier, and more satisfying out of life that's got *your name* on it—it's your growth journey ahead.

Key Takeaways

- If you don't take the lead and intentionally wire your brain for the things that really matter to you, then you will fall into the old way of being, which often leads to a stereotypical sedentary lifestyle that first began as a procrastination.

- Take the lead so the old way doesn't become your most dominant way of thinking and behaving. The way to do that is to leverage neuroplasticity before it's too late.

- Intentionally use your power to exercise your brain, gain new clarity, and create new growth experiences for yourself.

- The Rewire Retirement Method specifically deals with this purposefully, helping you gain clarity before taking outward action. It doesn't leave anything up for grabs. And if it is up for grabs, the old way is going to grab it very easily!

PART 2

Breakdown: The Rewire Retirement Method

"Intellectual growth should commence at birth and cease only at death."

—Albert Einstein

CHAPTER 6

Secret Weapon: The Magic of Micro-Stepping

The single most important ingredient for the Rewire Retirement Method to work successfully is all in one word: consistency. To get consistency, you need to use the magic of what I call "micro-stepping."

Micro-stepping is basically breaking down an action into incremental daily steps. Doing so is your surefire way to do the right things consistently.

Without micro-steps, negative patterns take over. Remember, that's the power of neuroplasticity. It can work for or against you. Which means the more clear and precise your daily micro-steps, the better—especially if it's a new topic or goal that you're tackling.

The trick is to leave no room for options to waver and bounce around in your head; therefore you won't fall victim to following your emotions and waiting to feel like doing something important. Don't allow your old lizard brain to take over!

This means intentional consistency is going to be your best friend. It's how your new, better-serving thought patterns can stick long enough and form new pathways in your brain. After the initial learning curve hump, the new way will eventually take on a momentum of its own. This consistency is how you create an upward trajectory filled with new and exciting growth experiences for the rest of your life.

A friendly reminder: if you don't actively convert your pre-retirement energy into your retirement life with intention, you leave it up to the already well-traveled neural pathways to become further entrenched.

Important for Gaining Clarity

On top of being conditioned for only external motivations, a big reason why a lot of people don't have crystal clarity about what they want their ideal retirement to look like is because they don't prod their brain for a consistent enough period of time. This is the exact reason why people who do a self-reflective process as a cram session experience only temporary results.

For instance, if you sit down and extensively journal about what you want to do and how you plan to achieve your ideal best retirement life all in one sitting, it doesn't always pan out the way you want. Even if it's a fancy vision board process, regardless of the format, the exercise often becomes a fleeting moment that doesn't take hold of any real momentum. As a result, you don't really gain clarity.

The process needs to include consistent and intentional daily micro-stepping to access that beautiful upward momentum and, therefore, true clarity.

Important for Engaging Micro-Steps

The same thing goes for taking outward action and engaging micro-steps. Lack of consistency and momentum are also why retreats, or similar condensed events, unleash only an initial swell of amazing emotions, actions, and ideas and are effective in the short term. Then you go back to normal life. The positive changes unfortunately don't stick because that positive momentum isn't built to last for the long haul.

Micro-stepping is your linchpin of implementing a positive improvement in life over the long term, be it a behavior, action, or thought pattern.

As a real-life personal example, micro-stepping is precisely how I gained clarity and founded Second Wind Movement back in 2018. Despite it being a really challenging and busy time in my life (just after my daughter was born), turning my passion into a reality became something that I just could not stop due to the power of micro-steps.

At the time, I was juggling a lot—a full-time marketing director role and caring for my first newborn—yet I was able to move forward with this passion that was growing in the background. I knew the magic of micro-steps (and went a bit overboard!) and committed to a 100-day micro-stepping challenge. These days, when I do micro-stepping challenges, I typically squeeze in 30-day sequences.

But this was something hugely important to me during a very tight period, as far as energy and time investment. By the time I finished 100 days of micro-steps, I had:

- Achieved my life coaching certification and started coaching older adults one on one

- Launched my business, built my website from scratch, and published eight blog articles

- Researched, written, structured, and recorded my full Rewire My Retirement program

I'm sure momentum took place early on (around day sixty-six), but regardless of intensity level, micro-stepping is the way for momentum to start seriously rolling. Truly, the right kind of positive inertia only grows with consistent and clear daily action.

It didn't matter how itty-bitty my daily micro-steps were (some days I could only muster up five minutes), I felt good about the cumulative movement forward. About midway through my micro-steps, I absolutely knew that my program was coming to full-fledged life with this mighty clarity and momentum standing behind it.

And it continues to work wonders across the board for all walks of life. You just need to gain clarity first.

Key Takeaways

- To achieve your best retirement life using the Rewire Retirement Method, you need consistency in both the "inward action" and "outward action" steps.

- To get that consistency, use the power of micro-stepping by breaking down your action items into clear, incremental daily steps. This allows you to build intentional inertia in one focused area.

- Engaging micro-steps daily and consistently *will* build momentum and progress so long as you take the time to gain clarity and exacting steps beforehand.

CHAPTER 7

Step #1
Gain Clarity:
Inward Action

Step #1 is to Gain Clarity by taking inward action and prodding your brain repetitively in a specific way that unlocks the deeper desires and possibilities from your subconscious. You will never find the answers outside of you; the clarity can only come by going inward. This is very much a brain hack. Do this *before* you engage in the real world, make big decisions, or tackle any series of actions.

The number one mistake I see people make as they transition into retirement is they "wing it" and live by trial and error. More specifically, they allow a bunch of floating ideas and emotions to take the lead, following the advice and suggestions of others, or simply doing what's popular (what they think they are "supposed to do"), only to be disappointed by the mismatch and drained of energy and motivation.

This is why I hear a lot of blanket statements, for instance, on the topic of Giving Back: "I'm burned out on volunteering" or "Volunteering is just not for me." But the truth is you just need to discover your own energizing way of sharing your unique gifts with others. This applies to any of the topics inside the 5 Rings of Retirement.

To avoid wasting any more time and energy on ideas and activities that aren't the right fit, you need to be crystal clear on both the big picture and the individual mini-goals that together make up your whole dream retirement life.

The way to do that is to focus on an inward self-discovery process and use the 5 Rings of Retirement as your basis for asking yourself the right questions about each topic.

I highly recommend simply going through each of the 5 Rings of Retirement one by one and heading deep into a writing exercise where you candidly journal ideas within each category, without judgment, so *all* of your ideas move out of your head and land onto paper. As simple as it sounds, journaling is a very powerful exercise, especially when you do it repetitively and freely (think stream of consciousness) with a specific topic and goal in mind.

Not only does research reveal there are numerous mental health benefits of journaling (including reducing stress, processing trauma, and deepening self-discovery),[1] but a recent study also shows stronger brain activity when putting pen to paper in comparison to writing on a tablet or smartphone.[2]

For more brainstorming juice, head back to chapter 4 with this new lens in mind. As you reread the 5 Rings of Retirement, jot down the ideas that come up as you ask yourself what you imagine your dream life to look like in this particular area. Again, do not judge what comes out (save that for much later). Simply follow the energy that *feels* good.

During your brainstorm, be as specific as possible, and pay extra attention to the ideas that conjure up energizing emotions. I call these "energizing breadcrumbs." They are your best clues for what's right for *you*.

As for the writing prompts, you can either ask yourself the same general question for each topic ("What does a level 5 in energy look like in my dream retirement life?"), or you can expand on it with follow-up prompts and organically follow the most energizing breadcrumbs as they arise.

Here's the important part: repeat the process the next day, and do the writing exercises for a consistent period of time for a series of no less than fourteen days.

In my fully guided Rewire My Retirement program, I've designed it so Step #1 extends over *two months*. That's how serious I am about gaining crystal clarity before taking any outward action. It's the best use of your precious time and energy. Over the course of *sixty days,*

I lead you through every question, prompt, and exercise needed to unlock the clarity from your brain each and every day. Basically, when it comes to gaining clarity on your innermost desires, dreams, hopes, wishes, and goals, it's worth getting into a consistent process so that no stone goes unturned. If you want a more reliable, methodical process, you can follow the program inside Rewire My Retirement. Just head over to secondwindmovement.com/rewire for details.

BONUS TIP: If you're one to try things on your own DIY-style, and you find yourself struggling to fill fourteen days' worth of journaling even after going through the 5 Rings of Retirement, try including these baseline Finding Clarity Questions on the next page to keep you moving.

FINDING CLARITY Q's

- What are your passions?
- What are your regrets?
- What's the biggest challenge you're facing?
- What are your strengths and biggest accomplishments?
- What are you most proud of?
- What's something you value most?
- Which core values do you want to pass on to your children and grandchildren?
- Choose three words to describe yourself
- In just three words, what's your philosophy for living?
- What core values do you want people to think of when they think of you?
- What inspires you the most?
- What's a significant event in your life that helped to define you?
- What do others say about you and who you are at your core?

Please don't complete the exercises all in one sitting. Continue a daily writing exercise practice for at least fourteen days.

Either way, to be consistent, a great rule of thumb is to spend twenty minutes per day actively probing your brain during your writing exercise. If you get stuck, just stick out the remainder of the twenty minutes and let it go for the rest of the day. Then, simply return to the exercise the next day and try it again.

The great news is, when you're consistent with Step #1, neuroplasticity does most of the work for you. It's like magic. The more you probe your brain, the more the topics marinate in your brain and create cumulative benefits. In other words, your subconscious releases details and aha moments during the remaining 23.3 hours of the day—most likely when you're not sitting directly in front of your writing exercise.

Why does it happen this way? Again, leave it to glorious neuroanatomy.

There's a two-inch system in your brain above your spinal cord called the Reticular Activating System (RAS). It filters in your senses (all but smell), connecting your subconscious to your conscious.[3]

The way to hack the RAS for your ideal retirement life is to be intentional and committed to actively probing your brain to gain clarity. This kicks the RAS into high gear, which then filters out the extraneous noise so the relevant juicy details can get to your conscious brain.

Let me give you a classic example of the RAS in action: You're shopping for a new car and begin researching options and become interested in a white convertible. Then you find yourself driving around town only to see more and more, lo and behold, white convertibles on the road.

That's the beauty of the RAS, and yes, you can absolutely use it to your advantage in Step #1—Gain Clarity of the Rewire Retirement Method.

If you're following the Rewire My Retirement program, you'll accomplish great clarity inside of two months. If you're doing it on your own, you'll *know* in your body when you gain clarity, particularly if you follow the Step #1 process for several weeks. As much as this is a brain process, your body will tell you.

You'll feel deeply excited with a strong sense of inner knowing in your gut. Physically, it can also feel like a tingling sensation within your stomach or chest, rising through your life force channel as you think about your great ideas. If this intuition-speak sounds a bit woo-woo to you, don't worry. You can rely on regimented steps and simply recognize your aha moments as a mental click that you've experienced in the past.

When that clarity is revealed, you are ready for Step #2.

Key Takeaways

- Step #1 is to Gain Clarity as your first inward action before taking any outward action.

- What most people miss is they look outward for the answers by either mimicking others' ideas, taking the advice of others, playing the comparison game, or skipping this first step altogether.

- As with all the steps, consistency is key. The more you prod your brain daily and consecutively with intentional, specific questions, the more the RAS in your brain will filter in the answers you're looking for.

CHAPTER 8

Step #2
Engage Micro-Steps:
Outward Action

Step #2 of Engage Micro-Steps is about taking focused outward action based on the clarity that you uncovered in Step #1. The best way to go about that is to use the trusty 5 Rings of Retirement framework to find out where exactly to put your focus first, then rely on the magic of engaging micro-steps to carry out those action items.

Let's find your first focal point by the following actions:

- Rate your energy level from 1 to 5 in each of the 5 Rings of Retirement.

- Which ring scored the lowest? That lowest-scoring ring is likely the area that needs your most attention right now.

- Choose one ring to focus on first. If it resonates, go with the lowest-scoring area first. If you're on the fence in between rings with the same score, pick one that sounds the easiest to tackle first.

RATE YOUR ENERGY LEVELS

Depleted   Neutral   Energized

1   2   3   4   5

5 RINGS OF RETIREMENT

? GROWTH   ? HEALTH   ? FINANCE

? COMMUNITY   ? GIVING BACK

Remember that you're simply integrating a new system into your brain, so starting small and easy is key. Once the inertia gets going the momentum will take you into the next area of focus, and you'll eventually get to the other Rings that also need your attention. The theme of this entire exercise is paring down, so choose one category only.

It looks as simple as this:

RATE YOUR ENERGY LEVELS

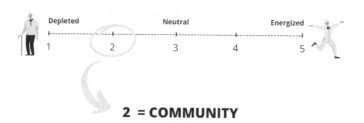

2 = COMMUNITY

After you select your single ring to focus on, it's time to create your micro-steps. To do this, we start broad and then get granular. Just follow this sequence:

- Within your single ring of focus, write down at least three mini-goals that would boost your energy to a level 5 in this area. Put another way, what do you need in your life for your energy level in this ring to significantly increase? Write down your ideas on a piece of paper.

- Next, pare down again and choose one of your mini-goals and circle it. For instance, if you choose "Community," your mini-goals might look like this:

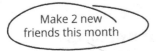

Make 2 new friends this month

Spend more time with 2 family members this month

CREATE MINI-GOALS

Attend 1 social activity per week

Reconnect with 3 old friends next month

Go out to lunch with a friend 1x a week

As over-familiar as it may sound, the next step is to turn your mini-goal into a proper SMART goal. This method is popular in corporations across the globe for a reason—it works. Again, we're here to keep things simply moving forward. As a reminder, a SMART goal is:

- **Specific:** turn hazy into clear concrete details

- **Measurable:** quantify it and set criteria

- **Achievable:** make sure it's not impossible

- **Relevant:** define a benefit or reason for reaching it

- **Timely:** set a date for achieving your goal

To continue our example, your SMART mini-goal might resemble:

- **S** – Be more socially active by meeting new like-minded people with similar interests.

- **M** – Get in front of at least five new groups of people to make two new friends.

- **A** – The goal seems realistic enough.

- **R** – Being social is healthy, stimulating, and enhances your sense of purpose.

- **T** – Do it within four weeks.

A mini-goal statement might reads something like:

My current "Community" mini-goal is to make two new friends within the next four weeks, so I can enjoy time with like-minded people with similar interests, which will be exciting, engaging, and healthy for me.

Now for your final step, which is where you outline your daily micro-steps. This is where you let yourself freely brainstorm and list out as many micro-steps as possible. The more you list, the better (shoot for a minimum of ten ideas). If any of the ideas sound daunting, then break them down into smaller micro-steps.

Here's where the most important part comes in: engage in one micro-step per day until your mini-goal is complete. Do not skip any days if you can help it. If you do, just pick up where you left off and continue your cadence of tackling one daily micro-step, never cramming to catch up. Keep in mind that some micro-steps are meant to be repeated and/or continued the following day until complete. Either way, you get the point: aim for a steady micro-stepping rhythm.

This even-keeled micro-movement is how to successfully engage your brain to stay focused and make real progress on something that matters to you—*consistently,* day after day.

Key Takeaways

- Step #2 is to Engage Micro-Steps and take outward action based on your newfound clarity. The process is intentionally simple, allowing you to build momentum and master consistency.

- Pick one focal point and select one Ring of Retirement to work on first by rating your energy level in each. Then write down at least three ideas that will boost your energy in this ring, and choose one as your focused mini-goal.

- Create your micro-steps by brainstorming a long, healthy list of action items, then add to them as you engage micro-steps and make progress.

- Most importantly, engage one micro-step daily (some will be repeat micro-steps). Don't stop until your mini-goal is achieved. Keep it simple.

CHAPTER 9

Step #3
Build Momentum:
Structure It In

The linchpin of the Rewire Retirement Method is to build momentum from the start. Step #3 of Build Momentum should begin right alongside Step #1. More specifically, as soon as you start the gaining clarity process and probe your subconscious brain for answers, be sure to dedicate time and space into your physical schedule to repeat the "inward action" practice several consecutive days in a row.

The tried-and-true way to do this is to stick to the 20-minute rule and get a good daily rhythm going. This way, no matter how busy or un-busy, scattered or focused, stressed or relaxed you currently are, there's a habitual way to keep your motivation moving forward.

113

The same thing applies to Step #2. As you take "outer action" you need to continue engaging micro-steps daily and consistently, which means Step #3—Build Momentum persists and doesn't skip a beat when you switch from "inward action" to "outer action." Put another way, when you finish your one mini-goal within one Ring of Retirement, repeat the process for each of the 5 Rings of Retirement.

And then keep going.

You may find more clarity along the way, and you may tweak and fine-tune your plans (in fact, expect it if you master this method). Just keep going.

You get the gist. It's a powerful process that gets wired into your system and then fires up from there. By the time you layer into your reality the initial pieces of your dream life one by one, your natural-born energy organically takes on an invigorating pulse of its own. This is called authentic personal growth.

Throughout the entire process of rewiring your brain, you'll come out the other side with a heightened awareness of:

- What intrinsically motivates you

- What energizes versus drains you

- Which micro-steps to take next

- Where to put your focus

- How to fit it all in

- A glorious new way of learning and thinking that feels so good

The importance of Step #3 is in dedicating time and energy to this method each day, intentionally building momentum. Basically, repeat this system as you grow, and bring it with you to your new heights.

There is no harm in repeating. In fact, honing this practice will only benefit you. No clarity will ever go wasted, and no ceiling will ever be reached as you continue to evolve and experience more and more of your most joyous, authentic, and vibrant life.

For instance, Steve, my Rewire My Retirement all-star student, went through his first round of daily micro-steps, gained clarity, then literally micro-stepped his way to his ambitious goal, which was to reach the top of Mt. Lassen for his seventieth birthday. He went through the program again and again to gain more clarity as he grew to great heights, each time fine-tuning his priorities and preferences. What once started as a solo mountain climbing priority turned into smaller hill hiking and flat-ground walking with others with the purpose of ministering and creating deeper human connections.

The point is to treat this process like a practice session of an important skill you want to master. Just like a pro basketball player treats repeat free-throws as the path to winning games, your repeat daily micro-steps in all three stages of the Rewire Retirement Method (and beyond) will only benefit you. Not to mention, it'll also benefit those around you.

If you want to add in another reliable way to securely build momentum, do this:

- Take advantage of your morning routine. When your willpower reserves are the greatest and your brain is coming out of a fresh theta wave, write down *when* you'll take your micro-step that day. You don't necessarily have to complete your micro-step in the morning, but jot down the time that you'll commit to doing it.

This process of separating your times—as in your time to "intend" versus your time to "act"—will take the guesswork out of planning your micro-step and stop it from lingering in your brain. It flies out of your head, lands onto paper, and routinely finds a clear space in your day (only twenty minutes on average) so that unreliable willpower doesn't have to.

Please note that your daily micro-step (doesn't matter if it's part of Step #1 or #2) does not belong on your to-do list. To-do items typically don't have an assigned calendar time, so micro-steps aren't a good fit.

Whether or not you love to-do lists, there are different types of people soaking in this book. Awareness is everything, so please check out how you'll integrate Step #3. Because momentum is invisible, people are likely to miss this very key part of the Rewire Retirement Method.

Some of you reading this book are motivated self-starters who will take this information and act fast. You'll head directly into your own brainstorm session following the 5 Rings of Retirement, and you'll try your best to stick to the twenty minutes per day brainstorm session until you experience enough energy surges from your newfound clarity. Then you'll quickly enter Step #2 and execute some activities to enjoy, hopefully with enough momentum to keep you going and growing.

Others will start and then . . . *stop.* Your initial brainstorm session will build some momentum but not enough consistent consecutive days of gaining clarity will take place, which means your best most optimized level of clarity won't happen. And then, your normal life (the life you had before reading this book) will eventually take hold again and simply resume.

And a third group of you will go for the quickest path and take advantage of the guided Rewire My Retirement program where everything is laid out for you over a three-month period, and you'll happily be well on your rewired way with built-in momentum.

There's yet one more subgroup for the "super learn-it-alls." You'll want private one-on-one coaching for the most hands-on, personalized growth journey. And I'm happy to offer that to those who really want and need it. The best part is you submit your daily exercises to me (in confidence), so I proactively get to know you in the background, which makes your coaching sessions that much more productive and effective.

My work as a life coach for older adults is my passion and my calling, and I do this day in and day out. I love helping successful people reach greater and greater heights, particularly when you're open-minded enough to embrace bigger dreams and really leverage the Rewire Retirement Method. I can see very clearly from my seat how to short-path your way to success, and then it's game on!

Be aware of which group you fall into and, more importantly, be intentional about where you'll invest your time and energy moving forward.

Key Takeaways

- Step #3 is to Build Momentum from the start, which means dedicating daily calendar time to your rewiring process. Ideally, work Step #1 and the initial part of Step #2 into your morning routine when your willpower is the greatest and your intentions are not hijacked.

- This consistency creates positive inertia in motion that allows you to continue engaging your dream life into your real life one micro-step and mini-goal at a time.

- You will only gain more clarity, confidence, and success by repeating and continuing the Rewire Retirement Method.

CHAPTER 10

Rewiring in Real Life Fast (aka the Right Way)

People enter the "seeking better" phase and begin exploring the Rewire Retirement Method from all walks of life. Truly.

- The pre-retirees with crazy-busy schedules, high-stimulators, and minimal time and attention to spare.

- The people who've been retired for years ping-ponging from one idea, place, person, and activity to the next, lacking priority or focus.

- The people (both pre-retired and retired) with too much time on their hands who find themselves procrastinating, feeling bored, and lacking motivation, energy, direction and engagement.

- The middle-ground people who are simply ho-humming through life. They can't complain, yet they keep playing the self-judging comparison game and subtly crave change and growth—and simply want more in life.

Doesn't matter if you're pre-retired, post-retired, or semi-retired. You can also toss in wildcards like illness, layoffs, loss, financial pressure, weather storms, relationship dynamics, relocation, vacations, visits, celebrations, weddings—you name it.

You get the idea. There are seasons of life and dynamically different ways of being.

And when there's such a varied set of daily paces, backgrounds, personalities, individual situations, and brain patterns (on top of life's swelling ebbs and flows), it's especially important to use a daily structure that meets you exactly where you are—anywhere, anytime.

Otherwise, the very conditioned "old way" easily takes over in your brain. Yes, even when you have all the right secret ingredients and steps laid out directly in front of you. Remember, this is very much a brain game.

Even with the wide range of individual factors, it's very possible to have a consistent daily structure. And *that intentional consistency* is going to carry you through any season.

The trick to a successful retirement structure (even if it includes work hours) is to have three to five basic buckets scheduled in, leaving enough room for elasticity, flexibility, and swap-outs.

In other words, have a general landing pad on your calendar for each category so you know where to put it, and include plenty of extra minutes as breathing room around each.

For instance, a skeleton daily structure could include these four category buckets:

- **Daily practices:** exercise, journaling, meditation, yoga, walks, reflections, personal development

- **Energizing me-time:** passion projects, outdoor activities, creativity, reading, rest, relaxation, free time, classes

- **To-do items:** chores, responsibilities, duties, doctor's appointments, grocery shopping, phone calls, admin tasks, house projects

- **Social time:** dinners, lunches, coffee meetups, visits, shows, social events, family, friends

As for calendar time, it could look something like this, where you place each item in a relevant bucket:

Morning routine	Daily practices	exercise, journaling, meditation, yoga, walks, reflections, personal development
Mid-morning	Energizing me-time	passion projects, outdoor activities, creativity, reading, rest, relaxation, free time, classes
After lunch	To-do items	chores, responsibilities, duties, doctor's appointments, grocery shopping, phone calls, admin tasks, house projects
Early evening	Social time	dinners, lunches, coffee meet-ups, visits, shows, social events, family, friends

Can you shift things around as your schedule, plans, and life dynamics change? Of course. Now you simply know what category was swapped out so it, too, can have a landing pad.

And where to include your Rewire Retirement Method? If you're following the above sample, it fits nicely (and quite effectively) into your daily practices within your morning routine.

Do you need to stick to each category so tightly that every minute is accounted for? No.

But here's an exception as a bonus tip where minutes do matter: Lock in your early morning and late evening minutes. It's worth setting a regular *wake time* and *bedtime* for the benefits of:

- **Avoiding getting sucked into screentime:** You'll benefit from setting a specific time to start and/or stop screentime, be it email, social media, news, or entertainment. According to PEW research, older adults aged sixty and over are spending more time in front of their screens than a decade ago.[1]

- **Getting regular sleep:** According to a study on sleep among the aging population, an alarming 40 to 70 percent of older adults have chronic sleep issues with nearly 50 percent being likely undiagnosed.[2]

Of course, tailor your structure to your current individual situation, but the point is the same across the board: a basic daily structure is how you can have it *all*, from freedom to obligation.

It's about including on your actual calendar, everything that's important to you *and* everything you both need and have to do.

Structure doesn't disappear in retirement. It may sound backward, but you need to schedule in free, spontaneous time. Yes, being more structured with your schedule gives you more freedom in your schedule. Just like you schedule in your vacations, schedule the small-scale versions into your at-home rhythm too.

Key Takeaways

- It's not superfluous to have a daily structure in retirement. To weather all the concurrent transitions in retirement, from learning how to spend down money to shifting your identity into your retirement role, a clear structure with built-in wiggle room is vital.

- To quickly rewire your daily life for optimal success, outline three to five core activity groups in your life, and give each a general time block in your day. Then list all the various items for each so you can see where to place every activity type.

- The best place to land the Rewire Retirement Method is in your morning routine under daily practices, with consistency still being the big priority.

PART 3

Avoiding the
Brain Traps

"The brain is like a muscle. When it is in use we feel very good. Understanding is joyous."

—Carl Sagan

CHAPTER 11

How to Kill Procrastination for Good

Simply put, you must eliminate procrastination by eliminating decision fatigue.

According to the American Medical Association, decision fatigue is "the idea that after making many decisions, your ability to make more and more decisions over the course of a day becomes worse."[1]

Too often, people don't do what they intend because there's the luxury of too many choices. Analysis paralysis is a real thing. In fact, known as the *paradox of choice,* coined by Barry Schwartz, when you have too many options, it causes you more stress.[2]

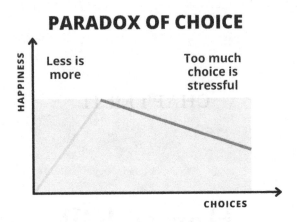

Which is why, if you're tackling the Rewire Retirement Method, you know that clocking in a daily gaining clarity session and then a daily practice engaging micro-steps removes that problem altogether. In fact, here's how each rewiring step helps reduce decision fatigue:

- **STEP #1—Gain Clarity:** When you probe your brain at the same time daily, it becomes a habit (and your RAS gets primed for clarity), creating less of a mental decision battle, especially over time.

- **STEP #2—Engage Micro-Steps:** When you reserve the morning period for your specific intention and you appoint a time for your daily micro-step, you remove extraneous decision-making for if, how, and when you'll fit in your daily micro-step.

- **STEP #3—Build Momentum:** When you structure in consistency from the start, the momentum of daily action takes a stronghold, turning your "intentional rewiring" into an everyday practice, replacing your habit of overthinking decisions and getting in your own way.

There's a theme here—intentional consistency creates intentional habit—that provides structure to your day-to-day life and drastically cuts down the amount of decision fatigue in your brain. It's a theme in line with brain hacking, and you can apply this same concept to anything and everything related to your compulsion to procrastinate.

More specifically, the trick for killing procrastination is to remove any grey-area decision-making and create an "IF-THEN" statement. Here's how:

Literally write down a statement that follows this simple format:

- IF I catch myself [insert your time stealer].

- THEN I will [insert a very simple, small action that creates positive inertia].

Then commit to following through every single time (which is why your "THEN" should be extremely small, physical, and doable).

Here are some examples:

1. IF I catch myself watching too much television, THEN I will get up, drink a glass of water, and refocus on one micro-step.

2. IF I catch myself scrolling too much on social media, THEN I will get up, walk outside, and water my garden.

3. IF I catch myself skipping my morning gym time, THEN I will drop and do twenty push-ups or sit-ups (and at the next opportunity, strive to solely get out the door).

4. IF I catch myself playing too many rounds of solitaire, THEN I will get up, walk straight to my to-do list, and commit to one quick activity.

You can also build in a backup time slot. Use these sparingly to avoid the habit of flaking on yourself:

5. IF I miss my 8:00 a.m. morning meditation, THEN I will meditate at 3:00 p.m.

Of course, your IF-THEN statement is personal and unique to your current habits, but the universal purpose is to eliminate grey-area choices causing daily decision fatigue and, hence, daily procrastination. The more specific, the better. It's all about executing a thought-pattern interrupt.

I hear phrases like this too often: *"I find myself just wasting a lot of time getting distracted and avoiding things, and then the day is gone."*

Unfortunately, that limbo state of analysis paralysis means you're susceptible to giving too much of your time to things like a television series, Netflix, Facebook, news, device games, or even checking email. Regardless of your time-sink format, there's likely an addictive screen tightly glued to your procrastination.

I highly recommend being proactive about this hack and completing the exercise now. Write down three relevant IF-THEN statements that you can rely on. Add more as you go through the rewiring process.

Key Takeaways

- End procrastination by ending decision fatigue. The paradox of choice causes stress, and analysis paralysis is a real thing. Both contribute to procrastination and being stuck in a retirement rut.

- To curb the mental load culprit behind procrastination, a powerful tool is the IF-THEN statement, which you prepare ahead of time for any thought and behavioral patterns you want to replace. The more specific the better.

CHAPTER 12

The Best Mindset (Because It Matters)

Micro-steps and momentum will get you through the Rewire Retirement Method swimmingly well, but if you really want to move upward fast, there's one mindset that'll quicken your pace: the Growth Mindset.

Dr. Carol Dweck coined the term and shares in her book *Mindset: The New Psychology of Success* that in a Growth Mindset, "people believe that their most basic abilities can be developed through dedication and hard work. Brains and talent are just the starting point."[1]

Of course, the other side of the coin is a Fixed Mindset where "people believe their basic qualities, like their intelligence or talent, are simply fixed traits. They spend their time documenting their intelligence or talent instead of developing them. They also believe that talent alone creates success—without effort."

In a nutshell, a Growth Mindset is believing that effort and hard work will develop your skills, talent, and intelligence. It's like believing in neuroplasticity. A Fixed Mindset is believing the opposite. It's not about the effort, but rather that people are simply born with or without a skill, talent, or intelligence level.

Do not undermine the power of the Growth Mindset, particularly as an older adult with more years of life under your belt. You've had more time on this planet than school-aged children to wire in some deep beliefs, and a common restricting belief is that you're old enough to be a know-it-all (or worse, you're too old to learn new things).

My favorite tip for adopting a Growth Mindset: *Be a learn-it-all, not a know-it-all.*

Also, follow these four key components:

1. **Seek challenges:** Paving new neural pathways and achieving meaningful goals will not come easy, so embrace the pitfalls as learning opportunities on the way to excellence.

2. **Focus on the process:** Savor your current stage. Look back at how far you've come if you need to.

3. **Accept feedback:** Rather than seeing it as strictly criticism, feedback can be productive and help you tweak and fine-tune as you strive and learn.

4. **Practice mindfulness:** Awareness is everything. Practicing mindfulness will help in *all* areas of your life, especially when it's done daily (oh those cumulative benefits).

Here's where we pull the benefits out of the classroom setting and place them smack-dab into the middle of retirement. A Growth Mindset:

- **Helps you gain clarity:** What's important here is to be completely open-minded and not assume anything about yourself as you prod your brain for clarity, which is especially important as you begin the inward self-exploration process in Step #1—Gain Clarity.

- **Helps you engage micro-steps consistently:** By focusing on the process (versus the outcome), you'll build resilience and continue engaging micro-steps even if your streak breaks, which means you'll have less all-or-nothing thinking and not give up as you might in Step #2—Engage Micro-Steps.

- **Boosts your cognitive health:** The more you learn, the more you exercise your brain and create new neural pathways. You now know it too well; your brain follows the "use it or lose it" principle.

- **Makes you a more interesting human:** You're more likely to engage in great conversations about your new and exciting growth experiences, as opposed to repeating the stereotypical "same ole same ole" as you age. More interesting = more authentic friendships.

All of this goes hand-in-hand with exploring retirement as the beginning of a big growth journey. Keep in mind that growth doesn't have to mean crazy productivity or even constantly chasing a tangible goal.

You get to define your individual growth, and the Rewire Retirement Method will match you up to the things that authentically feel good and fulfilling in your current life stage. For some it may mean spiritual growth; for others it may look like learning how to relax and soothe your nervous system. And yet for others it may be a combination of work and play.

Whatever it may be, your growth will continue to evolve over time and will weave in deeper human connection. My intent is that you continue to become more and more of your authentic self and align with people, places, activities, and events that naturally energize you.

Key Takeaways

- A Growth Mindset is the belief that you can develop a skill, talent, or knowledge base through your effort and dedication. This fuels your retirement growth and success.

- A Fixed Mindset, believing that you have no control over these things, will keep you stuck in a retirement rut.

- The fact that neuroplasticity exists proves that you're wired for growth. You just need the right system in place. Use the Growth Mindset to your advantage, and become a learn-it-all instead of a know-it-all.

- To adopt a Growth Mindset, follow these four tips: seek challenges, focus on the process, accept feedback, and practice mindfulness.

- Retirement-related benefits of adopting a Growth Mindset include gaining clarity, engaging micro-steps consistently, boosting your cognitive health, and becoming a more interesting human.

CHAPTER 13

Recognizing and Overcoming Silent Blocks

It's one thing to read these words: "a rewired life is an exciting life with dynamic, rich, and robust growth." It brings to life amazing new experiences that you deep down want to partake in your lifetime. It's another thing to take action and consistently follow the Rewire Retirement Method system until you start to unleash your dream life into your reality.

Sometimes, though, the action doesn't happen. But it's not because of lack of willpower or clear intent. It's simply because of deeply rooted blockages. For some people, it's a deep-seated, ingrained pathway where you (often unknowingly) cling onto patterns that no longer serve you. Even if you are aware of unhealthy thought and behavioral patterns, your lizard brain likes comfort, and comfort makes it extremely difficult to maneuver out of.

But maneuvering out of the old way is well worth the effort. Remember, if you don't convert your floating post-career energy into something intentional and energizing, it converts *itself* into some form of mental health risk, often depression or anxiety . . . which is running rampant at the moment.

Sadly, a recent study found that a staggering 45 percent of older adults agree that normal aging includes depression, and over 50 percent of those with clinical level mental health risks do not seek help.[1]

Here's my quick PSA: You don't have to accept poor mental health as part of the aging process. And it's not something that you just snap yourself out of.

If you or anyone you know is suffering from poor mental health, please get help. There are numerous ways to seek professional guidance these days, whether it's remote or in person, a group or private setting, or with a counselor, therapist, or life coach. Find a healing setup that resonates with you.

You have more control over the way you age than you think. In fact, only 25 percent of your longevity is dependent on genetics; the other more significant 75 percent is dependent on external factors *in* your control, such as your environment, lifestyle choices, and behavior.[2] Please do not accept unhealthy beliefs as part of the normal aging process, even if they're status quo.

We have a family friend, Eve, and I love talking about her because she's the classic example of how much your environment and lifestyle choices make a difference. She is a tiny woman who is so *mighty*. Proof? She continued surfing well into her nineties.

Surfing aside, I'm compelled to share two very common blocks that repeatedly come up in private coaching sessions. To help you overcome the subconscious, repeated neural pathways that stubbornly clench onto the old way, consider these tips that could set you and your brain free.

Silent Block #1: Relationships

I don't need to tell you that relationships are one of the toughest dynamics to navigate, mainly because you're in control of only your part of the deal, sometimes forcing you into topics, situations, or decisions you normally wouldn't if you were flying solo.

More often than not, your spouse plays the biggest role in either supporting or detracting you from your growth path. As a life coach, I frequently help students and clients clearly define:

- Your activities

- Your partner's activities

- Couple's activities together

As simple as these buckets are, it's worth sorting out your own priorities within your growth journey so you can protect and focus on them. This also creates a clear view of where and when to invest your energy (and where to expect your partner's energy). It also helps you figure out whether it's shared effort into the couple's category, only limited guidance into your partner's arena, or most of your energy into your own experiences.

A second helpful practice that works wonders for people is keeping a gratitude journal dedicated to your spouse. As in, write daily about the things you appreciate in your partner. Go deep, shallow, big, small, present, past, and future hopes—all of it. Just try to do it on a daily basis.

Gratitude is a buzzword for a reason: it works. It's the antidote to fear, anger, anxiety—basically, any low-frequency emotion that you want to elevate. So imagine the outcome of consistently softening the lens of your spouse inside your brain, day-after-day. There are only real benefits here.

There's no sugarcoating it. As time goes on, divorce rates among older adults over 50 (aka gray divorce) is soaring. So much so that the gray divorce rate was 8.7 percent in 1990, 27 percent in 2010, and an astounding 36 percent by 2019.[3]

If your marriage is suffering, consider seeking help—as a couple or for you individually. A stressful relationship dynamic will hinder each party's growth potential and life satisfaction.

Side note: One hundred percent of the people who improve themselves also improve their relationships. This makes complete sense because the dynamic between a better version of you and any other human *has* to shift and improve. The biggest side effect of adopting the Rewire Retirement Method is your relationships improve 100 percent of the time.

Silent Block #2: Older (Personal) Baggage

Head back into your past, well before any marriage, and you'll likely find emotional scars that you've been carrying forth, likely to manifest deep into later adulthood. It may sound far-fetched, but the healing of these childhood wounds is directly related to your potential for and rate of growth in retirement.

More often than not, no matter how conscious you are about your childhood wounds, the tissues in your body physically keep the survival patterns ongoing.

Doesn't matter if it's trauma with a capital *T* or lowercase *t*, trauma is common. Sadly, as many as 70 percent of US adults have experienced some type of traumatic event at least once in their lives.[4]

Couple this fact with the typical narratives of past generations and you'll pinpoint the source of self-limiting beliefs, which have been handed down since at least the Traditionalists, Silent Generation, and Greatest Generation of the early 1900s. The growth-stunting beliefs that I'm referring to might sound something like:

- *"There's a war. We're poor, and we might run out of money and food, so we need to keep working and saving. If I stop working, I'll feel guilty."*

- *"If you have an emotional issue, soldier up, suck it in, and move on."*

- *"What will people think if they find out? Just snap out of it and don't mention it."*

- *"Crying is a sign of weakness. You need to be strong."*

- *"Work comes way before play. You earn the right to relax."*

While these aren't exact scripts and the narratives are mostly subtle and subconscious, the message is quite significant, and the impact is very real.

Beliefs like these often manifest in adulthood and continue through later adulthood in the form of self-abandonment, overworking, burnout, low self-worth, people pleasing, over-giving, stress, addiction, lack of self-confidence, difficulty with decision-making, analysis paralysis, anxiety, depression, clutter, judgment, fear of change, codependence, and on and on.

You get the gist. These are merely coping mechanisms that you needed to survive as a child, but you no longer need them to *thrive* as an older adult.

Unintentionally, your parents and grandparents likely passed on some generational hand-me-downs that foster a sense of "stuckness" (hence, the low stats for people seeking professional help).

Here's the number one tool my students and clients use on a daily basis to be the one to stop unhealthy generational patterns and snap the brain out of any *extra* stuckness stemming from the past: *mindfulness.*

Yes, this single word encompasses hundreds of formats, speeds, shapes, sizes, and styles, but one thing is universal. Mindfulness helps you go inward for stillness as a way to capture presence and connect with your real essence.

What's the big idea? When you go inward to meet your authentic self, you will begin to uncoil the conditioned coping mechanisms. Which means in your brain, you create and nurture a new way.

At the root of this block is a need for self-love, self-care, self-esteem, and self-connection. If any of this resonates with you (even if it's deep down), consider any one or combination of these scientifically proven daily practices to nicely complement your Rewire Retirement Method process:

- Meditation (again, there are several hundreds of paths to take here)

- Yoga, stretching, tai chi, chi gong, neigong

- Walking in the woods or connecting with nature

- Hot baths or ice baths

- Journaling, self-reflection, contemplation

- Mirror work, mantras, affirmations, prayer, dedications

- Breathwork, somatic experiencing, EFT tapping

Basically, anything that gets you out of your head and into your body. The goal is to trigger your parasympathetic nervous system (rest and digest) instead of your sympathetic nervous system (fight-or-flight) more regularly. It's a nurturing process.

Over time, the benefits of mindfulness exceed most people's (sometimes judgmental) expectations, and they will for you too. Just pick a practice that resonates and add it to your daily rituals.

Key Takeaways

- **Silent Block #1** is within your relationships. Focus on getting clear on your own growth priorities versus your partner's. If you're experiencing relationship issues, keeping a gratitude journal dedicated solely to your partner will work wonders.

- **Silent Block #2** is emotional wounding and triggers stemming from deep within your past. They create coping mechanisms that served you in childhood yet stunt you in later adulthood. Whether they are induced by childhood trauma or by inheriting a parent's traditional narrative, silent blocks are very common, and overcoming any past wounds will unblock you from stuckness. Mindfulness helps you triumph over these conditioned emotions.

- Seeking help is extraordinarily beneficial, especially for successful people at the top. Whether it's through coaching, counseling, therapy, or mentoring, find a program that resonates with you the most. There's a trusty short path to where you want to be.

Conclusion

"If you're always trying to be normal
you will never know how amazing
you can be." —Maya Angelou

When it comes to taking the next steps, as I mentioned at the end of chapter 9 (Step #3—Build Momentum), there are three basic types of people. For each group, I share my honest life coaching advice on what to do next.

1. **DIY Self-Motivators:** You'll finish this book and immediately get started on your own brainstorming writing exercises using the 5 Rings of Retirement. You'll strive for consistency over a period of time, make some headway in gaining clarity, and do a decent amount of building momentum.

   What to do: If this is you, great. Just keep going. Keep in mind the pro tip I share throughout this book: focus on keeping the process simple and consistent. Without complicating anything, simply strive for excellence and own your single growth process.

For instance, it's more than okay to repeat Step #1—Gain Clarity. I actually highly recommend it for fine-tuning and filling in more detail (and growth). Remember that no clarity will ever go lost. In fact, you will only gain more nuanced, exciting ideas as you continue and repeat this system. After all, you're designed to evolve and develop over the years, so please don't let the years deep into your future be any different.

You're not here to settle for stagnancy. If you do find yourself coming to a growth lull, which does happen (undoubtedly, life gets in the way and eternally ebbs and flows), please reach out for help. You now know you have more options and a better way.

Knowledge of more options removes fear; knowledge of a direct short path to your dream life removes decision fatigue.

2. **Start-Stoppers:** You'll find initial motivation and set off on your own version of gaining clarity, but then get distracted and pulled in another direction. Gaining clarity won't make the top of your priority list for long enough, and the preexisting wiring in your brain's limbic system (lizard brain) will resume its course.

   This means you may find yourself ping-ponging around from one thing to the next, lacking focus and, again, feeling spread thin on energy and time. And that's okay. You're not alone, and this is pretty common.

   What to do: Remember that it's a brain game, where the old wiring is just a bit stickier. In fact, a lot of people cultivate such a conditioned mindset that it stems way back to childhood (often wired in from trauma). When this goes unresolved for decades, the coping mechanisms simply become more stubborn and manifest in later adulthood.

Even if it's not stemmed from childhood trauma, hardcore brain conditioning can get tangled pretty good from a demanding work environment (think managerial role with profit margin pressure, personnel issues, and tight deadlines).

It doesn't matter what's at the root; there is a way out. The old way just needs to be rerouted with stronger consistency and momentum, and a deeper look at the self-priority, self-love, self-care aspect. Call it what you want, but this is where help is *very* beneficial. If anything, for the sake of saving you tons of time and energy.

Seriously Consider Help: If you find yourself being swung right back into the rut of a life on autopilot, understand that it's time to really consider your options for outside help, be it the fully guided Rewire My Retirement program, a life coach, therapist, counselor, or any combination. No matter what kind of help resonates the most, it's worth it and you're worth it.

3. **Fast-Track Achievers:** You'll hop right into the Rewire My Retirement program and follow the guided step-by-step process every day until you achieve the results you're looking for. You'll simply follow the system, trust the process, and let neuroplasticity do the work for you in all three stages: Gain Clarity, Engage

Micro-Steps, and Build Momentum. Within three months, you'll integrate consistency directly into your system and enjoy an upward trajectory with enough positive inertia to carry you onward indefinitely. It's just a matter of how high and fast you want to go, which is a personal choice.

What to do: Choose either the self-study or fully guided Rewire My Retirement program. Some will choose the quickest most personal path to success and opt for the private coaching sessions (as long as there's availability, of course) to complement the program.

Remember it's about giving yourself permission to shine above the norm, to grow into all your possibilities. It's about prioritizing invisible things like joy, satisfaction, self-actualization, passion, and your sense of purpose. There's a direct process for achieving your dream retirement life. Let yourself receive it without getting in your own way.

How to Get Help

It's important to continue your momentum beyond the last page of this book. *Keep going. Keep seeking.*

You're reading this book for a reason, you know there's more to life than limiting societal norms, and you want to grow into your best life as your authentic self. Not just conceptually, but in reality.

To help you continue your growth journey, I've included some extra helpful resources and additional training.

Also, if you want to cut to the chase and quickly and successfully implement the steps laid out in this book in a foolproof step-by-step way, I've included information and a link on how to join the fully guided **Rewire My Retirement** program. There are multiple offerings from self-study to VIP coaching options, so please see the details below.

A Deeper Dive into the 5 Rings of Retirement

In this video episode, I walk you through a deeper look at the 5 Rings of Retirement to help you proactively plan out more than just the financial aspect of retirement. Pair it with the Ultimate Retirement Checklist (download the PDF right below the video), and you'll be well on your way to gaining clarity with one clean document.

secondwindmovement.com/5rings

Finding Clarity Workbook

One of the most challenging parts about gaining clarity is not knowing what questions to ask, let alone come up with the answers. Download your Finding Clarity Workbook, and follow along this video lesson to get the most out of these important exercises and prompts. It's a great start for the inward journey.

secondwindmovement.com/clarity

Join the VIP Facebook Group

Join this exclusive group of other like-minded people who are aspiring toward their ideal retirement lifestyle. This free community was created just for you to see what it really means to build a lifestyle you love.

facebook.com/groups/secondwindmovement

Second Wind Movement Blog

For continued learning and reading, head to Second Wind Movement's blog, which provides a well of educational articles published weekly. The content is categorized by the 5 Rings of Retirement framework and is designed to help older adults improve their health and relationships, nurture their purpose and passions, and more.

secondwindmovement.com/resources

Second Wind Movement YouTube Channel

To watch educational and engaging videos, subscribe to Second Wind Movement's YouTube channel, where you'll find a variety of video content that sheds light on various topics in the 5 Rings of Retirement. New episodes are published weekly, and you'll also find the popular "50 People Over 50" interview series.

youtube.com/@CynMeyerSecondWindMovement

Join the Rewire My Retirement Signature Program

I am always looking for the next success story to share. Your success has the potential to inspire so many others. If you want accelerated results, please join the Rewire My Retirement fully guided program. This is your most personalized, step-by-step, and efficient way to achieve a more meaningful and exciting retirement. We offer a range of options, from self-study to VIP coaching programs, to help as many people as possible achieve their dream life.

Now is your time to thrive, and I want to help you!

secondwindmovement.com/rewire

Notes

Chapter 2: A Modern Retirement Reality

1. Pedro Mateos-Aparicio, Antonio Rodríguez-Moreno, "The Impact of Studying Brain Plasticity," www.frontiersin.org/articles/10.3389/fncel.2019.00066/full.

2. US Bureau of Labor Statistics American Time Use Survey, Wall Street Journal, Mar 2023.

Chapter 3: The Top 3 Challenges Retirees Face

1. Ursina Teuscher, "Change and Persistence of Personal Identities After the Transition to Retirement," www.researchgate.net/publication/43078611.

Chapter 4: The 5 Rings of Retirement

1. Greg Miller, "A Busy Brain Is a Healthy Brain, Intellectually challenging hobbies may help prevent Alzheimer's," www.science.org/content/article/busy-brain-healthy-brain.

2. Shirley Leanos, MA, Esra Kürüm, PhD, Carla M Strickland-Hughes, PhD, et al., "Retracted and replaced: The Impact of

Learning Multiple Real-World Skills on Cognitive Abilities and Functional Independence in Healthy Older Adults," www.academic. oup.com/psychsocgerontology/article/75/6/1155/5519313.

3.   Peter A Bath, Dorly Deeg, "Social engagement and health outcomes among older people: introduction to a special section," www.ncbi. nlm.nih.gov/pmc/articles/PMC5547666.

4.   Fadia T Shaya, PhD, MPH, Viktor V Chirikov, MS, C Daniel Mullins, PhD, et al., "Social Networks Help Control Hypertension," www.ncbi.nlm.nih.gov/pmc/articles/PMC3580229.

5.   Leland Kim, "Loneliness Linked to Serious Health Problems and Death Among Elderly: UCSF Researchers Find Social Factors Play Major Role in Older Adults' Health," www.ucsf.edu/news/2012/06/98644/loneliness-linked-serious-health-problems-and-death-among-elderly.

6.   Alison R Huang, David L Roth, Tom Cidav, et al., "Social isolation and 9-year dementia risk in community-dwelling Medicare beneficiaries in the United States," J Am Geriatr Soc. 2023, www.pubmed.ncbi.nlm.nih.gov/36628523.

7.   William J Chopik, "Associations among relational values, support, health, and well-being across the adult lifespan," Department of Psychology, Michigan State University, www.onlinelibrary.wiley.com/doi/abs/10.1111/pere.12187.

8.   Alzheimer's Association, "2023 Alzheimer's Disease Facts and Figures," www.alz.org/media/Documents/alzheimers-facts-and-figures-infographic.pdf.

9. National Council on Aging, "NCOA–Falls Prevention Conversation Guide," www.patientcarelink.org/ncoa-falls-prevention-conversation-guide.

10. Kirk L English, Douglas Paddon-Jones, "Protecting muscle mass and function in older adults during bed rest," www.ncbi.nlm.nih.gov/pmc/articles/PMC3276215.

11. Sovianne ter Borg, Sjors Verlaan, Jaimie Hemsworth, et al., "Micronutrient intakes and potential inadequacies of community-dwelling older adults: a systematic review," British Journal of Nutrition, 2015, www.pubmed.ncbi.nlm.nih.gov/25822905.

12. Kathleen B. Watson, PhD, Susan A Carlson, PhD, Janelle P Gunn, MPH, et al., "Physical Inactivity Among Adults Aged 50 Years and Older," www.cdc.gov/mmwr/volumes/65/wr/mm6536a3.htm.

13. Emily Brandon, "7 Misconceptions About Retired Life," US News, 2011, www.money.usnews.com/money/retirement/articles/2011/10/11/7-misconceptions-about-retired-life.

14. Emily A Greenfield, Nadine F Marks, "Formal Volunteering as a Protective Factor for Older Adults' Psychological Well-Being," www.academic.oup.com/psychsocgerontology/article/59/5/S258/669124.

15. Sara Konrath, Andrea Fuhrel-Forbis, Alina Lou, Stephanie Brown, "Motives for volunteering are associated with mortality risk in older adults." Health Psychology, 2012, www.doi.org/10.1037/a0025226.

16. Eurofound, Anja Ehlers, Monika Reichert, Gerhard Naegele, "Volunteering by older people in the EU," www.data.europa.eu/doi/10.2806/1748.

17. SSM Health, "The science behind kindness and how it's good for your health," www.ssmhealth.com/blogs/ssm-health-matters/november-2022/the-science-behind-kindness.

18. AARP, "Almost Half of Americans Fear Running Out of Money in Retirement," 2019, www.aarp.org/retirement/planning-for-retirement/info-2019/retirees-fear-losing-money.html.

19. Alicia Adamczyk, "$1 million isn't enough to retire on in comfort, many Americans say," Fortune, 2023, www.fortune.com/2023/04/17/comfortable-retirement-requires-saving-more-than-one-million.

Chapter 5: The #1 Problem with Rewiring

1. Dr. Ken Dychtwald, "Life's Third Age," Age Wave, www.agewave.com/what-we-do/educational-programs/lifes-third-age.

2. TJ Shors, LM Anderson, D M Curlik, II, SM Nokia, "Use it or lose it: How neurogenesis keeps the brain fit for learning," www.ncbi.nlm.nih.gov/pmc/articles/PMC3191246.

3. Healthy Brains, "You are your brain," Cleveland Clinic, www.healthybrains.org/brain-facts

Chapter 7: Step #1—Gain Clarity: Inward Action

1. Margarita Tartakovsky, MS, "6 Journaling Benefits and How to Start Right Now," Healthline, www.healthline.com/health/benefits-of-journaling.

2. University of Tokyo, "Study shows stronger brain activity after writing on paper than on tablet or smartphone," ScienceDaily, 2021, www.sciencedaily.com/releases/2021/03/210319080820.htm.

3. Joseph H Arguinchona, Prasanna Tadi, "Neuroanatomy, Reticular Activating System," StatPearls Publishing, 2023, www.ncbi.nlm.nih.gov/books/NBK549835.

Chapter 10: Rewiring in Real Life Fast (aka the Right Way)

1. Gretchen Livingston, "Americans 60 and older are spending more time in front of their screens than a decade ago," Pew Research Center, 2019, www.pewresearch.org/short-reads/2019/06/18/americans-60-and-older-are-spending-more-time-in-front-of-their-screens-than-a-decade-ago.

2. Brienne Miner, Meir H Kryger, "Sleep in the Aging Population," Sleep Med Clin., 2017, www.pubmed.ncbi.nlm.nih.gov/28159095.

Chapter 11: How to Kill Procrastination for Good

1. Sara Berg, MS, "What doctors wish patients knew about decision fatigue," AMA, 2021, www.ama-assn.org/delivering-care/public-health/what-doctors-wish-patients-knew-about-decision-fatigue.

2. Barry Schwartz, *The Paradox of Choice: Why More Is Less.* (Harper Perennial, 2005).

Chapter 12: The Best Mindset (Because It Matters)

1. Dr. Carol Dweck, *Mindset: The New Psychology of Success.* (Ballantine Books, 2007).

Chapter 13: Recognizing and Overcoming Silent Blocks

1. Rapid Report, "Mental Health Has Bigger Challenges Than Stigma," Mental Health Million Project 2021, Sapien Labs, www.

mentalstateoftheworld.report/wp-content/uploads/2021/05/Rapid-Report-2021-Help-Seeking.pdf.

2. World Health Organization, "World Report on Ageing and Health," www.iris.who.int/bitstream/handle/10665/186463/9789240694811_eng.pdf.

3. Susan L Brown, I-Fen Lin, "The Graying of Divorce: A Half Century of Change," J Gerontol B Psychol Sci Soc Sci., 2022, www.ncbi.nlm.nih.gov/pmc/articles/PMC9434459.

4. C Benjet, E Bromet, EG Karam, et al., "The epidemiology of traumatic event exposure worldwide: results from the World Mental Health Survey Consortium," Psychol Med, www.ncbi.nlm.nih.gov/pmc/articles/PMC4869975.

About the Author

Cyn Meyer is the creator of the Rewire My Retirement program and a modern certified life coach committed to helping older adults turn their retirement years into their best years, full of purpose and passion. She founded Second Wind Movement in 2018 as a valuable resource dedicated to older adults who are striving for healthy, active, and engaged retirement lives. Every publication in her content library is educational and based on thorough research and successful application in real life. The material in her blog articles, YouTube videos, workbooks, and coursework span across the topics in the 5 Rings of Retirement.

My Mission, Your Journey

Everyone deserves fulfilling retirement years.

Sadly, this isn't always the case. I've experienced a lot of loss and death in my life, and I don't believe the majority of those who passed had a chance to live out fulfilling lives. The reality first shook me when I started playing music in retirement homes. I saw early on what happens with a sedentary lifestyle post-retirement and at the end of life.

Then I saw this at age sixteen when I lost my aunt to cancer. Her passing instilled in me a deep fear of aging without purpose—a feeling that has stayed with me throughout my life, especially after experiencing a great number of losses since then. After witnessing the brevity of people's "retirement honeymoon period" while serving in the financial services industry, the poor impact of society's aging stereotypes became too clear.

The cognitive health and brain impact shook me as well. Both of my grandparents passed, touched by Alzheimer's, which happens to one out of three at the end of life.

And then there's my dad. Despite surviving a brain surgery and near-death experience in 2011, he fell back into old habits of worry and duty, fearing retirement would leave him bored and purposeless.

These experiences drove me to delve deep into neuroscience.

I began coaching older adults one on one in 2018 and committed my life's work to finding ways to help people achieve fulfilling retirement lives through the power of brain plasticity and tailored life coaching tools.

The Rewire Retirement Method, rooted in neuroplasticity, is my answer to the fear of purposeless aging and goes well beyond your typical financial planning. It's a scientific system designed to help you embrace retirement as an exciting new growth journey, not a stereotypical time to wind down and settle into stagnancy.

My mission is simple: to help you live a vibrant, purposeful retirement life because you deserve nothing less.

 cynthia@secondwindmovement.com

 secondwindmovement.com/rewire

youtube.com/@CynMeyerSecondWindMovement

facebook.com/secondwindmovement

Made in the USA
Monee, IL
08 March 2024

54680253R10095